TOKYO

KAIJU ATTACKS

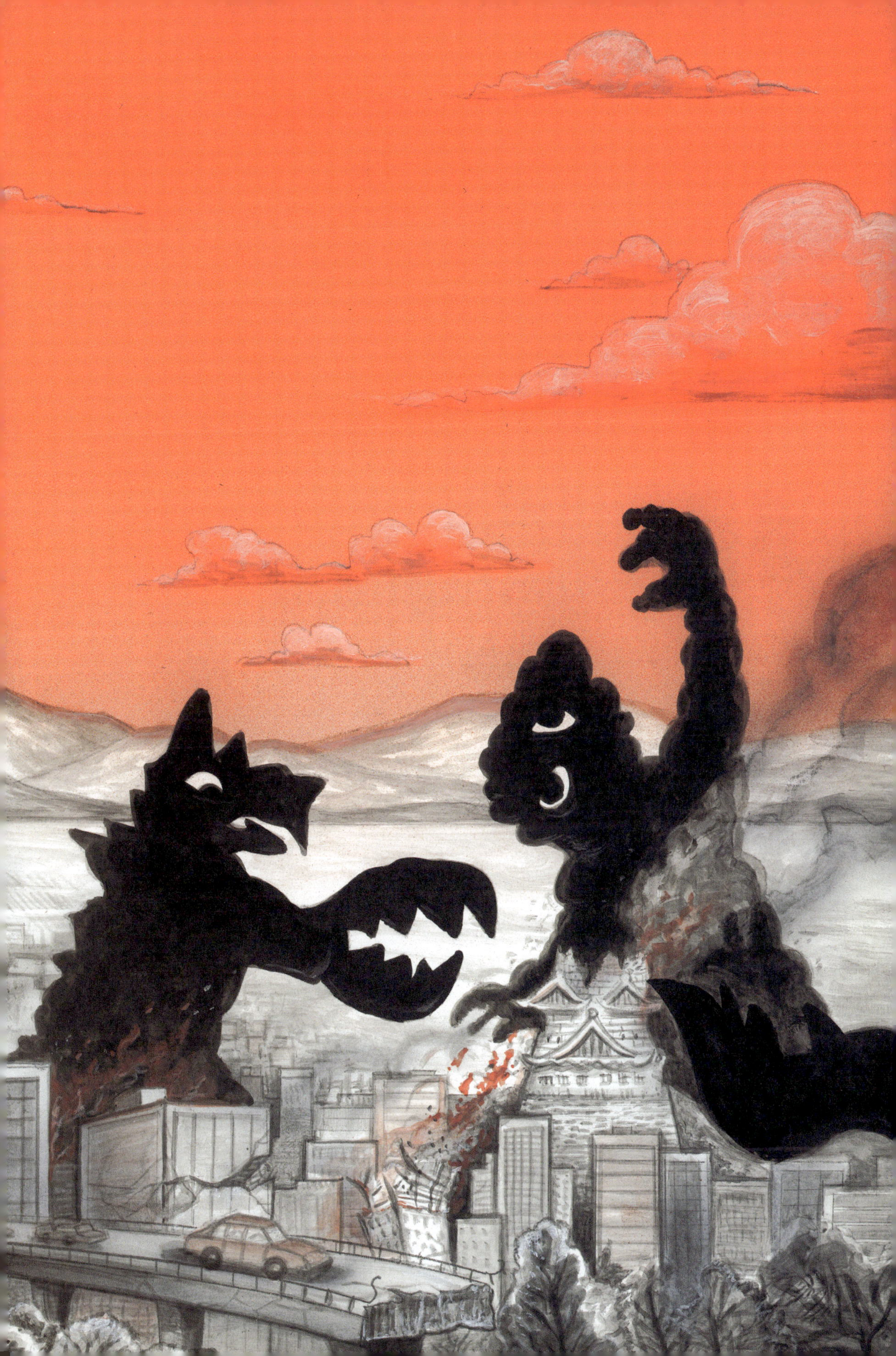

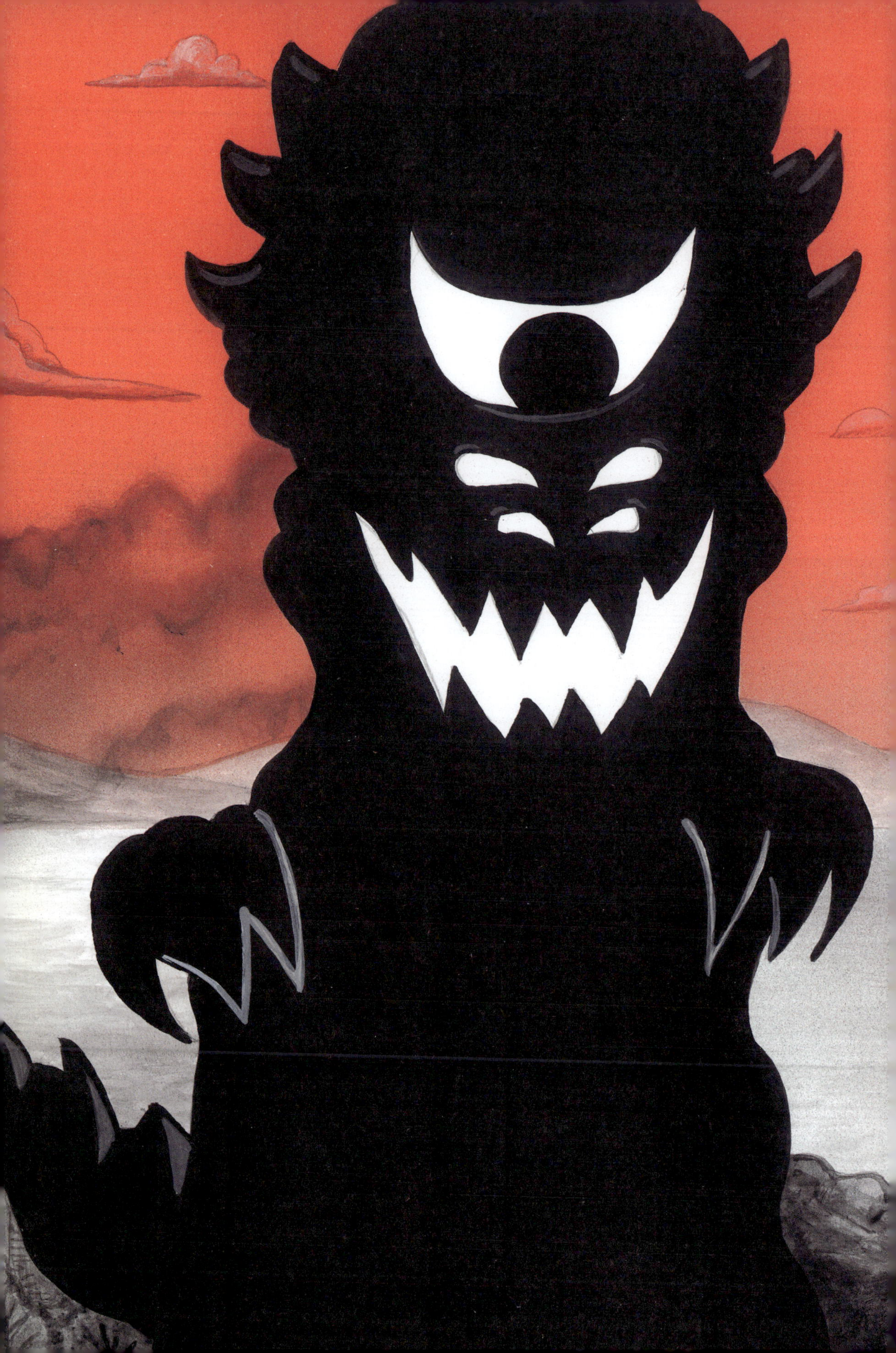

KILLER KAIJU MONSTERS

怪獣

STRANGE BEASTS OF JAPANESE FILM

Ivan Vartanian

Including original art by

Mark Nagata

Ryohei Tanaka

Keisuke Saka

Ariel Martin

Shinji Abe

Naritada Shintani

Sakabashira Imiri

Collins Design
An Imprint of HarperCollins Publishers

Killer Kaiju Monsters
Copyright © 2009 by Goliga Books, Inc.

All rights reserved. No part of this book may be used or reproduced in any manner whatsoever without written permission except in the case of brief quotations embodied in critical articles and reviews. For information, address Collins Design, 10 East 53rd Street, New York, NY 10022.

HarperCollins books may be purchased for educational, business, or sales promotional use. For information, please write: Special Markets Department, HarperCollinsPublishers, 10 East 53rd Street, New York, NY 10022.

First published in 2009 by
Collins Design
An Imprint of HarperCollins*Publishers*
10 East 53rd Street
New York, NY 10022
Tel: (212) 207-7000
Fax: (212) 207-7654
collinsdesign@harpercollins.com
www.harpercollins.com

Distributed by
HarperCollins*Publishers*
10 East 53rd Street
New York, NY 10022
Fax: (212) 207-7654

Library of Congress Control Number: 2009925395

ISBN: 978-0-06-165579-1

This book was produced by Goliga Books, Inc.
Editorial and Art Direction by Ivan Vartanian
www.goliga.com

Layout by Yuko Shoji for Karera Design
www.karerano.com

Production and Edition Coordination by
Rico Komanoya/ricorico

Pages 1 to 6, Illustrations by Mark Nagata

The author would like to express humble thanks to Mark Nagata, Shinji Abe, Ariel Martian, Keisuke Saka, and Ryohei Tanaka, the artists who created original artwork for this volume. Many individuals also provided invaluable advice and feedback, including Lester Fykes, William Fleming, Asako Nambu, Lesley A. Martin, Kyoko Wada, Yo Miyamoto, and Justine Parker. Thanks to Hiromoto Mihara of Billiken Shokai, Professor Yoshihiko Sugimoto of Kyoto University, and Yoshiaki Yamato of NHK.

Printed in China
First Printing 2009

Page 21: *Godzilla* © 1954 Toho Co., Ltd. All rights reserved. Page 22: *Ghidorah, the Three-Headed Monster* © 1964 Toho Co., Ltd. All rights reserved. Pages 24–25: © 2009 Toho Co., Ltd. All rights reserved. Pages 26–27: *Godzilla* © 1954 Toho Co., Ltd. All rights reserved. Pages 28–29: *Godzilla* © 1954 Toho Co., Ltd. All rights reserved. Pages 30–31: *Godzilla: Tokyo SOS* © 2003 Toho Pictures Inc. All rights reserved. Page 33: *Godzilla Raids Again* © 1955 Toho Co., Ltd. All rights reserved. Pages 34–35: *Godzilla Raids Again* © 1955 Toho Co., Ltd. All rights reserved. Page 37: *Mothra vs. Godzilla* © 1964 Toho Co., Ltd. All rights reserved. Pages 38–39: *Godzilla Final Wars* © 2004 Toho Pictures Inc. All rights reserved. Pages 40–41: *Mothra vs. Godzilla* © 1964 Toho Co., Ltd. All rights reserved. Page 42: *Godzilla vs. Hedorah* © 1971 Toho Co., Ltd. All rights reserved. Pages 44–45: *Godzilla vs. Hedorah* © 1971 Toho Co., Ltd. All rights reserved. Pages 46–47: *Godzilla vs. Hedorah* © 1971 Toho Co., Ltd. All rights reserved. Pages 48–49: *Godzilla vs. Hedorah* © 1971 Toho Co., Ltd. All rights reserved. Page 51: *Ghidorah, the Three-Headed Monster* © 1964 Toho Co., Ltd. All rights reserved. Pages 52–53: *Godzilla vs. Gigan* © 1972 Toho Co., Ltd. All rights reserved. Pages 54–55: *Destroy All Monsters* © 1968 Toho Co., Ltd. All rights reserved. Page 57: *Rodan* © 1956 Toho Co., Ltd. All rights reserved. Pages 58–59: *Rodan* © 1956 Toho Co., Ltd. All rights reserved. Page 61: *Godzilla vs. Megalon* © 1973 Toho Co., Ltd. All rights reserved. Pages 62–63: *Godzilla vs. Megalon* © 1973 Toho Co., Ltd. All rights reserved. Page 64: *Godzilla vs. Gigan* © 1972 Toho Co., Ltd. All rights reserved. Pages 66–67: *Godzilla vs. Gigan* © 1972 Toho Co., Ltd. All rights reserved. Pages 68–69: *Godzilla Final Wars* © 2004 Toho Pictures Inc. All rights reserved. Page 71: *Son of Godzilla* © 1967 Toho Co., Ltd. All rights reserved. Pages 72–73: *Godzilla Final Wars* © 2004 Toho Pictures Inc. All rights reserved.

Trademark Notice: Godzilla, King Ghidorah, Mothra, Rodan, Anguirus, Hedorah, Megalon, Gigan, Jet Jaguar, Minilla and the character designs are trademarks of Toho Co., Ltd. All rights reserved.

Disclaimer: This publication is not sponsored or otherwise endorsed by Toho Co., Ltd.

Pages 74, 76–79: © 1966 Kadokawa Pictures, Inc.

はじめに Intro: Beware, Tokyo! 010–015

紙製怪獣 Paper Craft by Keisuke Saka 016

怪獣達 Kaiju Dossier 020–079

機能比較 Kaiju Abilities 017–019

解剖図 Kaiju Cross Sections by Shoji Ohtomo 080–089

注目獣 Eyezon by Mark Nagata 090–093

玩具 Soft-Vinyl Figures 094–107

怪獣切絵 Cut Drawing by Ryohei Tanaka 108–115

怪獣図画 Kaiju Illustration 116–127

怪獣×妖怪 Kaiju vs. Yokai by Shinji Abe 128–144

怪

KAI

獣

JŪ

はじめに
Beware, Tokyo!

by Ivan Vartanian

Kaiju is the Japanese word for "monster." While the word had earlier been in common use in Japan, from the 1950s onward the term took on a particular significance, referring specifically to the special effects movies and television series of the postwar era. The unique qualities of kaiju (as distinguished from Western monsters and the culture that grew around those characters) are the principal focus of this volume. With the explosion of gamer culture, urban vinyl, and the burgeoning interest in Japan's contemporary visual arts, kaiju has emerged as a concept traversing from Eastern to Western culture along the same route traveled by *manga* and *anime* (as distinct from comic book and cartoon). As such subculture vocabulary is appropriated by the lexicon of contemporary art and popular consciousness, keywords such as kaiju represent a recontextualization of ideas, both culturally and historically. Kaiju Big Battel, for example, is a live wrestling event held in various American cities by hobbyists who duke it out in a ring dressed in cardboard costumes inspired or modeled on existing kaiju characters. Exports such as the radioactivity-induced Mutant Ninja Turtles and shape-shifting Pokemon (Pocket Monsters) are more popular examples of kaiju-sytle character design. At the same time, recent horror films such as *The Ring* and *Ju-on* feature the dispossessed type of monsters known as *yokai*, a companion genre to kaiju. In the realm of contemporary art, Kenji Yanobe's Godzilla sculpture or Takashi Murakami's artist collective Kaikai Kiki also make direct references to kaiju themes. The name of Murakami's group is a play on "kiki kaikai," meaning something monstrous and creepy. Indeed, the rejected subtext of a lot of contemporary Japanese culture is revisited like some latent psychosis made manifest.

The word "kaiju" itself carries a lot of meaning. The first Chinese character is read as *kai*, and means mysterious, unknown, or surprising. In combination with other characters, such as 怪異・怪火・怪奇・怪死・怪談・怪盗・怪物, it often has a negative association, meaning otherworldly. In combination with the character for fire, it denotes a mysterious fire; with the character for death, it means death from a mysterious cause. Other combinations include: gruesome, ghost story, a phantom thief, or a ghost. In the final section of this volume, it is paired as the second character of 妖怪, read as *yokai* (pronounced with a long vowel), meaning "ghost" or a creature taking a monstrous shape. The character 獣, read as *ju* (pronounced with a long vowel) when in combination with another character, means "beast." It refers most commonly to a beast covered with hair and is used for words related to animals both wild and domesticated. *Kai + ju* (怪獣) together translate as "monster." There is a striking similarity between kaiju and the original connotation of "monster," which has its origins in the Latin "monstrum," a divine omen or warning indicating misfortune. The most important gleaning from the characters is that of the mysterious, the gruesome, and the spirit world. The phrase is best understood in the context of Japanese folklore.

In film and television productions of postwar Japan, kaiju are large, brutally powerful creatures that are largely revamped versions of dinosaurs. The most commonly representative of them is Godzilla. In these story scenarios, most kaiju cannot be defeated with contemporary weapons and possess powers that are inscrutable in the eyes of science—special powers such as emitting heat rays from the mouth, flying at supersonic speeds, shape-shifting, or communicating telepathically. They are also commonly referred to as *dai-kaiju* or giant-kaiju. While these kaiju characters are wholly fictitious, they borrow legends of demons and spirits prevalent in Japanese culture. The introduction of such primitive and chaos-inducing beings into modern-day Tokyo is a clash of paradigms: the older, agrarian culture in sync with nature and steeped in folklore and ritual at odds with the achievements of industry and modernization.

Meanwhile, in the West, the film monster can be seen as a study in contrast to monsters from Japan's film world. King Kong, for instance, is a giant gorilla. Based on our understanding of dinosaur behavior, the creatures depicted in *Jurassic Park* are essentially acting true to form. The title character of the *Predator* movies is a cyborg creature who hunts human prey in forests—the larger threat to civilization is contained within the confines of the forest. The same is true of the creature in the *Alien* franchise, contained within a ship, the human body, or another planet. Where the threat is Tokyo, Osaka, or Nagoya, on the other hand, are identifiable locales with readily recognizable landmarks. Using the cities as the stage for these monster attacks makes it all the more apparent that the urban development of Japan in the postwar period is an integral component to kaiju narrative. In comparison with the monsters of Western films, kaiju are developed (to a limited degree) along the same lines of character development as their human counterparts. As opposed to being an unreasonable (and even random) threat, kaiju have a backstory that contextualizes their motivations for destruction. Almost without exception this motivation relates back to humans, making them culpable participants in the ensuing destruction and havoc. In many cases, Kaiju are brought to life through nuclear testing or extensive environmental pollution that is a direct consequence of unchecked human behavior.

The first wave of kaiju popularity was set off by the gargantuan success of *Godzilla* in the mid-1950s. Within six months' time, Toho, the studio that produced the film, released a follow-up. This pitted the first film's title character against another kaiju, Anguirus, who also resembled a prehistoric creature brought back from extinction. Seeing Toho's success, other studios, such as Toei, followed suit with similar kaiju films. What helped establish the popularity of the genre were the special effects, known as *toku-satsu*. *Tokusatsu eiga*, or special effects movies, drew in the theatergoers, but on a more fundamental level there was great difficulty in advancing the narrative of a feature-length film with action scenes. In many ways, *tokusatsu eiga* of this era—the late 1950s to the late 1960s—were essentially one film told from two perspectives: that of the humans caught in the cross fire and that of the kaiju. The actions of the human actors unfolded on one level and the special effects happened on another. It is no surprise that the movie's director and special effects director were given separate and equal credits in these early kaiju films.

The studios were able to bridge this gap to some degree through the use of intermediary figures, such as the twin girls in the Mothra features who communicated with the kaiju telepathically or Minilla, Godzilla's diminutive, adopted child.

The Toho Champion Festival (1969 to 1978) was a long-running film festival held to coincide with spring, summer, and winter school recesses. The main feature was a Godzilla film (either a rerelease of an older film or a new title), coupled with a sequence of previously aired television episodes. (The television shows aired in the theaters were not limited to the kaiju-related genre but also included anime.) Young boys were the main demographic and target audience for the production companies. The actual viewership was broader in age range. The human characters introduced in the films commonly included a boy or several boys. At times, the kaiju defended these human characters from threat.

In addition to the Godzilla and Gamera films and spin-off productions, other series of note include the *Daimajin* series (Toei), three films all made in 1966 whose title character is a spirit force that inhabits and animates a stone figure. *Toei Super Hero Fair* (1993–1995) is a series of three films by Toei. *Yosei Gorath* was a 1962 Toho science-fiction production about an out-of-orbit star on a collision course with Earth. The "yo" in *yosei* is the same character as the "yo" of *yokai*—referring to a spirit. *Atragon* or *Kaitei Gunkan* was a 1963 Toho special effects film based on a series of manga illustrated by Shigeru Komatsuzaki.

Tsuburaya Productions

Any discussion about *tokusatsu-eiga* begins with Eiji Tsuburaya, who was involved with the special effects direction of the first *Godzilla* movie and whose name would become synonymous with special effects movies and television series through his production company (also called Tsuburaya). The company's mid-1960s series *Ultra Q* followed by their color production *Ultraman* series, helped establish the television genre of hero-versus-kaiju production. The series pitted Ultraman against an onslaught of kaiju.

With the adaptation of the special effects kaiju to the small screen, the role of the scientist and his moral dilemma was replaced with the introduction of a superhero, most notably Ultraman in the Tsuburaya production of the same name (1966–1967). The *Ultra-Q* television series featured laboratories with enormous vegetables and plants capable of solving food supply issues and mysterious occurrences of materials falling from outer space. The struggle was simplified to a battle on par with a tug-of-war, pitting superhero against the kaiju menace.

Character Design

The cross sections in this volume were inspired by the work of Shoji Ohtomo, who was also an editor, science-fiction writer, and journalist. In the 1960s and 1970s his duotone illustrations in *shonen manga*, periodicals for young boys, as well as his editorial work made him an influential figure in the kaiju fiction world. In collaboration with legendary director Eiji Tsuburaya, he was active in establishing the details of kaiju, aliens, and scientific weapons. During the kaiju boom of the 1960s, his cross sections communicated corporeal reality to the characters, earning him the title of "Kaiju Hakushi" (Dr. Kaiju). Meanwhile, the panorama fight scenes were inspired by Shigeru Komatsuzaki, Noritsuna Maemura, and Takashi Minamimura—artists regularly engaged by the Tsuburaya studio. Tohl Narita is the artist who created the original design of Ultraman and numerous iconic kaiju of the television series. It is worth mentioning that Narita's work was inspired by surrealist artists. There is also an absurdist subtext to the television adaptation of the kaiju films, on a par with American television series such as *The Outer Limits* (1963–1965) and *The Twilight Zone* (1959–1964). The kaiju films and television series also inspired a legion of licensed soft-vinyl toys, which thereafter became playthings for generations of Japanese. The Bullmark, in particular, was the brand name that become synonymous with kaiju.

The yokai are spirit beings that take on a variety of forms, animating mundane objects such as tea kettles or appearing as ghouls (frequently female), usually with some gruesome characteristics such as long hair or one eye. Filmgoers in the West were treated to a classic adaptation of the yokai with the film *The Ring* (2002), a remake of the 1998 Japanese film based on the novel by Koji Suzuki. Sadako slithers out of a well and peers at her victims with one eye through a curtain of black hair. In contrast, the kaiju, while they do not possess gender, outwardly behave in a more masculine manner and their form of attack follows suit—an exchange of force. The yokai are more about terror and their powers have a more psychological basis rather than the imminent physical threat posed by the kaiju. They are also distinguished by their appearance. Where the kaiju is a very "real" blood-and-guts concoction of gnashing teeth and furious roar, the yokai are less tangible, sometimes appearing without feet or with elongated necks. In comparison, the kaiju generally maintain a consistent core silhouette resembling a dinosaur. There are certain kaiju that change shape or exist in multiple copies. Indeed, it is only the multiple nature of certain of these monsters which would explain the logic of a recurring kaiju with the same identity.

The split between kaiju and yokai genres as they appear in narrative construction—either in film, fantasy novels, or games—happened in the postwar period. Concurrent with this split was the introduction of the hero and the television productions. The advent of the hero allowed for a continuity within a series of television episodes. Episodes were built around the conflict between good and evil, a far simpler and accessible narrative conceit than the larger themes featured in film productions (Japan's international relations in a postwar context, environmental damage resulting from industrial development, or the rising threat of nuclear destruction). The role played by science in providing a rational perception of the world and its phenomena was often confounded by these creatures which exceeded human understanding. The spirit forces that terrified humans with abject horror are wholly absent from the postwar kaiju genre. Unanswered questions still abound, but at least modern science can supply methods of classification to provide some security. The introduction of the hero and the heroine—who battle the kaiju or are set with the task of stopping their rampages—is a major idea introduced in these postwar productions (particularly in television), leading most notably to *Ultraman* and the *Masked Rider* series.

The brute force that these kaiju exert to topple buildings and sow panic and fear among people and their governments cannot be emphasized enough. The very byproducts of our societies' advances have produced the seeds of their own destruction. At the same time, these destructive and terrifying beings are regarded in another manner as well. As displayed by Shigeru Mizuki's universe of "Gegege no onitaro," there is a playful subtext to the characterizations of the yokai that make them endearing. While such a quality is not as overt with *tokusatsu kaiju*, there is certainly a quality that appeals to audiences. The combination of a spirit force related to Japan's agrarian past and the perils of society in modern times distinguishes the kaiju from their Western monster counterparts. There are numerous kaiju varieties, such as *kougai kaiju* (environmental pollution kaiju), *uchuu ninja kaiju* (space ninja kaiju), *misairu chou-juu* (missle super beast), *denki kaiju* (electricity kaiju), and others. As late as the 1960s, the distinctions between kaiju and yokai (as well as that between Japanese and Western monsters such as Frankenstein, Werewolves, or King Kong) were less pronounced. In the years since, however, the differences between kaiju and yokai are more or less clear, while at the same time a cultural line has been drawn between monsters of the East and West. (This could be a mere matter of territorial licensing rights and the protection of copyrights.)

Kaiju as Metaphor
The fictional devastation visited upon Tokyo in *tokusatsu eiga* (special effects movies) of the 1950s is on par with the plagues that consumed an earlier, more agrarian version of Japanese society. Natural phenomena such as tsunami, sandstorms, or pestilence were made manifest in the form of spirits that lived within nature, drawing from the same life force that also yielded crops. This idea relates to animism, the attribution of a soul to plant life, inanimate objects, and natural phenomena. The subtext of early *tokusatsu eiga*, such as *Godzilla* (1954), is a lament for the loss of connection to nature. Once there was a respect for the land, demonstrated by countless regional ceremonies and rituals that were meant to safeguard the well-being of villagers and farmers and ensure bountiful crops. The folklore of these earlier generations was richly populated by mysterious creatures, such as *kappa* (a frog-like creature), *kamaitachi* (a weasel-like demon), *tanuki* (mischievous raccoons), as well as ghouls and freakish ghosts. The modernization of Japan and the expansion of its cities prompt broad speculation on the changing nature of Japanese society and the identity of its people. As civilization expanded, a threat remained. The kaiju that attack modern Japan are a modern equivalent of the spirits and demon forces that tossed about the Japanese of yesterday. A series of photographs taken by Eikoh Hosoe from 1964 to 1969 titled "Kamaitachi" shows *butoh* dancer Tatsumi Hijikata performing for the camera in the nothern region of Japan's mainland. The dancer's erratic (and even comic) movements and gestures—leaping into the air, digging himself into the group—represent the shift in paradigm between the agrarian world of Japan

before the war and the culture during the war. With the larger scale of our society there is a need for a larger scale of danger. In other words, the kaiju attacks on the city are emblematic of the greater horror of being separated from nature. Advances in science and technology radically altered the Japanese way of life and uprooted a people from their natural habitat. More to the point, the presence of nuclear energy and nuclear weapons in *Godzilla*, as well as the awful threat it poses to humankind, is an unmistakable morality play. This put a spotlight on the figure of the scientist and his role in facilitating these technological developments. The scientist is faced with a moral dilemma: How can a scientist conduct research that has the potential for awful consequences? To what extent can a scientist take responsibility for his inventions and discoveries? These questions remain relevant today.

紙製怪獣

Paper Craft

Karakuri Kaiju by Keisuke Saka

Toy makers in Japan have been fashioning elaborate mechanisms to animate dolls and models since the 17th century. These constructions are known as karakuri and what makes them remarkable is how all the moving parts are encased within the figure itself. What seems like an ordinary doll seems to come alive with the pull of a cord. The complexity of action and gesture of which these *karakuri* figures are capable is elaborate. They can serve tea, descend stairs, ride a horse, or perform simple magic tricks. This attempt to recreate the movements of people is also exhibited in Sony's robotic pet AIBO and Honda's ASIMO. Paper craft artist Keisuke Saka follows this tradition with the model included here and has incorporated a mechanism in the figure. Build it to find out what it can do.

Kaiju Paper Model Instructions
Tools: Scissors or Craft Knife, Ruler, Glue, Stylus, Pencil
- Before cutting pieces out, score the fold lines with a stylus or a blunt instrument. Press gently to indent the paper. Do not pierce the paper. Scoring helps the paper fold neatly and makes the model work better.
- Cut parts out carefully along cut lines. Smaller pieces may require the use of a craft or X-acto knife. Cut circles out precisely by holding the craft knife steady and turning the paper.
- Fold parts before applying glue. Note the fold type before folding. Hill folds (dotted lines) have the fold at the peak and valley folds (dashed lines) have the fold in the valley. Curved parts are created by laying the piece flat and rolling a pencil across it until the paper curls.
- Apply glue thinly and evenly with a toothpick on shaded areas. White school glue works best.

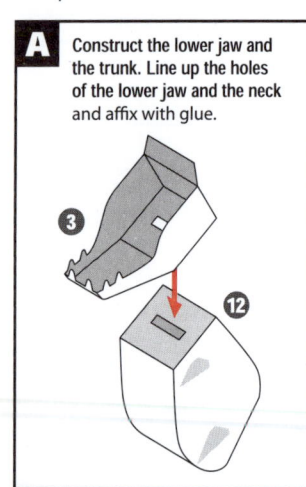

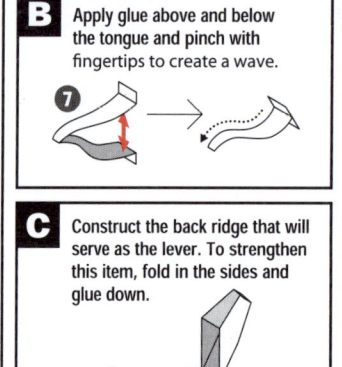

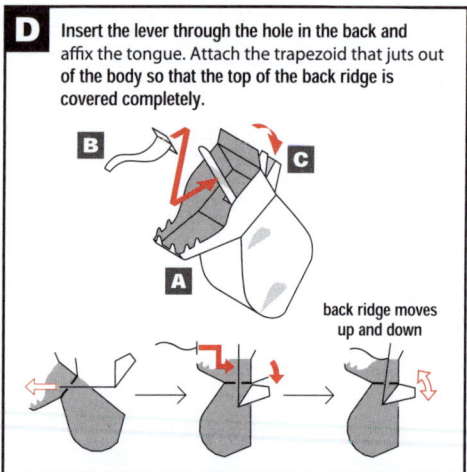

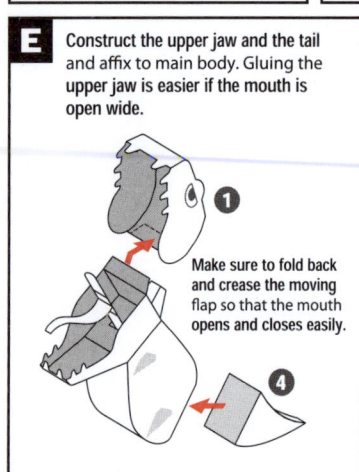

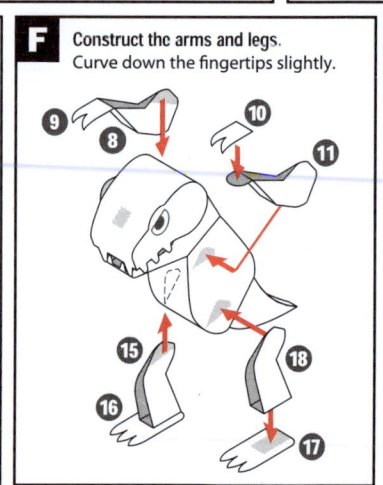

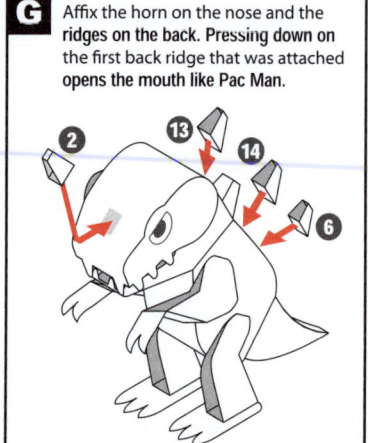

A Construct the lower jaw and the trunk. Line up the holes of the lower jaw and the neck and affix with glue.

B Apply glue above and below the tongue and pinch with fingertips to create a wave.

C Construct the back ridge that will serve as the lever. To strengthen this item, fold in the sides and glue down.

D Insert the lever through the hole in the back and affix the tongue. Attach the trapezoid that juts out of the body so that the top of the back ridge is covered completely.

back ridge moves up and down

E Construct the upper jaw and the tail and affix to main body. Gluing the upper jaw is easier if the mouth is open wide.

Make sure to fold back and crease the moving flap so that the mouth opens and closes easily.

F Construct the arms and legs. Curve down the fingertips slightly.

G Affix the horn on the nose and the ridges on the back. Pressing down on the first back ridge that was attached opens the mouth like Pac Man.

機能比較
Kaiju Abilities
Icons by Ariel Martian

複数
MULTIPLES
Some kaiju exist in multiple exact copies or are brought back as later models (generally more mechanical versions of their former selves).

放射性
RADIOACTIVE
The potential for widespread, destructive power. Most kaiju are brought into being through some connection with nuclear radiation. Nuclear tests in particular are a common cause for creating kaiju.

奴隷にする
MIND CONTROL
While uncommon, the ability to control minds is possessed by certain kaiju. Some kaiju also have the power to communicate telepathically (even with humanoids).

飛行力
FLIGHT
Even though a character such as Gamera is wingless, a giant turtle is capable of flying up to speeds of Mach 3. The same is true of Hedorah, who is able to fly at high speeds as well, despite a lack of wings or clearly defined propulsion mechanism.

巨大化
MAGNIFICATION
Shifting between different sizes of the same form allows kaiju to compact themselves for easy travel or expand to make a colossal entrance.

属性
AMPHIBIOUS/SUBTERRANEAN
By far the most common origin of kaiju is the ocean, followed by some dwelling below the Earth's surface. Hedorah can also change shape depending on exposure to water—shifting between a giant, tadpole-shaped kaiju to a legged surface warrior, and even taking to the air.

敗戦・復活
DEFEAT
Not all battles have a fatal ending. More often, kaiju are sent back where they came from so that they may fight again another day. When a kaiju does perish, it is always dramatic.

悲鳴
SCREECH ABILITY

A distinct muscial motif can signal the imminent entry of a kaiju, as can a particular screech. In the case of Anguirus, his screech is so powerful that its reverberations put cracks in the structure of the Osaka castle.

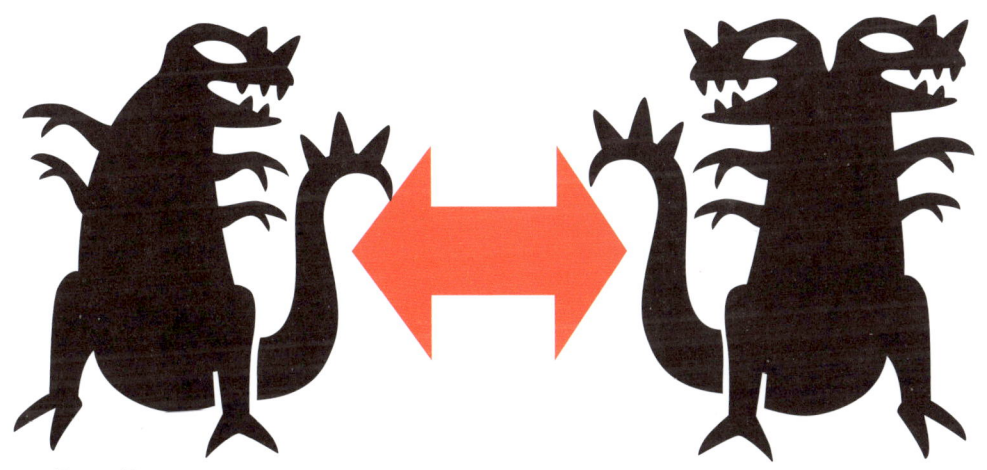

変身
SHAPE SHIFTING

Not unlike the developmental metamorphosis of reptiles and insects, kaiju can also change shape to suit a given situation and extend their abilities. Mothra, in particular, exists in two states: larva and imago. Rarely does this kaiju undergo a transformation of state within one film.

友獣
FRIEND/FOE TURNED FOE/FRIEND

Kaiju pitted against one another in one film regularly become allies in another. In the case of Gamera, with the exception of the debut film, he is a hero to young boys.

ゴジラ
Godzilla

Released in 1954, *Godzilla* launched a long series of films pitting kaiju against kaiju, leaving wreckage strewn across Japan's major cities in the process. Its star would come to be known as the King of Monsters. Yet how Godzilla come into existence—or *back* into existence—established a narrative model that was often used throughout the course of kaiju pro-ductions. Nuclear testing brought about a catastrophic change in a naturally existing creature. In Godzilla's case, according to paleontologist Kyohei Yamane (played by Takashi Shimura), the beast lived from the Jurassic period to the Cretaceous period and developed from a subaquatic crustacean to a land-dwelling being. Its ferocious form, however, is the result of multiple exposures to radiation from hydrogen bombs—or so the scientists theorize. The original movie poster (page 21) includes the tagline "Hydrogen Bomb Giant Kaiju Movie." This revisiting of the "sins of the father" is a thinly veiled metaphor for the destruction caused by the atomic bombs that were detonated in Hiroshima and Nagasaki at the close of World War II. The scenes of Tokyo's decimation evoked memories still quite fresh in viewers at the time and the subtext of the film was certainly not lost on adults. Rather than being a didactic tale about the excesses of human power, the narrative is more a clash between Japan's prewar and postwar identities and the modes of life they represent.

The name "Godzilla," according to the story, comes from the legend of the fictitious island Ootoshima. The release of the sixteenth film in 1984 dispensed with all the backstory from previous releases except for the first one and changed the monster's height to eighty meters. (Godzilla was originally fifty meters tall and stayed that way through the 1975 release of the fifteenth film in the franchise, *Terror of Mechagodzilla*.) With the release in 1991 of the eighteenth film, *Godzilla vs. King Ghidorah*, we learn more details of the monster's origins. Namely, it was a Godzillasaurus dinosaur living on the remote island of Ragosu in the Southern Sea when ocean testing of bombs on the Bikini Atoll produced radiation that caused the monster to morph into a kaiju.

As Godzilla achieved iconic status both domestically and abroad, the kaiju went through numerous permutations of shape as well as personality. Where Godzilla represents nothing but destruction in the first films, it is later seen as a defender of humans against other kaiju, somewhat of a hero, a parental figure, and portrayed as an isolated and dis-inherited creature. This character's ability to play all these roles shows how these films allow viewers to identify with and even cheer for kaiju. Indeed, kaiju narratives as a genre distinguish themselves in how much compassion they elicit from the audience despite the monster's awesome threat.

Original movie poster for *Godzilla* (1954).

Production Company: Toho | **STATS Height:** Up to 100m **Weight:** Up to 60,000 tons **Flight speed:** N/A **Origin:** Irradiated Godzillasaurus from Bikini Atoll | **Powers:** Atomic ray / Nuclear pulse / Super regeneration / Magnetic electricity force

水爆大怪獣映画
ゴジラ
ゴジラか、科学兵器か、驚異と戦慄の一大攻防戦！
放射能を吐く大怪獣の暴威は日本全土を恐怖のドン底に叩き込んだ！
宝田明
河内桃子
平田昭彦
志村喬
製作 田中友幸
脚本 村田武雄
監督 本多猪四郎
撮影 玉井正夫
美術 北猛夫
美術 中古智
録音 下永尚
堺左千夫
村上冬樹
山本廉
榊田敬二
鈴木豊明
馬野都留子
菅井きん
笈川武夫
林幹
恩田清二郎
高堂国典
小川虎之助
照明
音楽
特殊技術
東宝株式会社 製作・配給

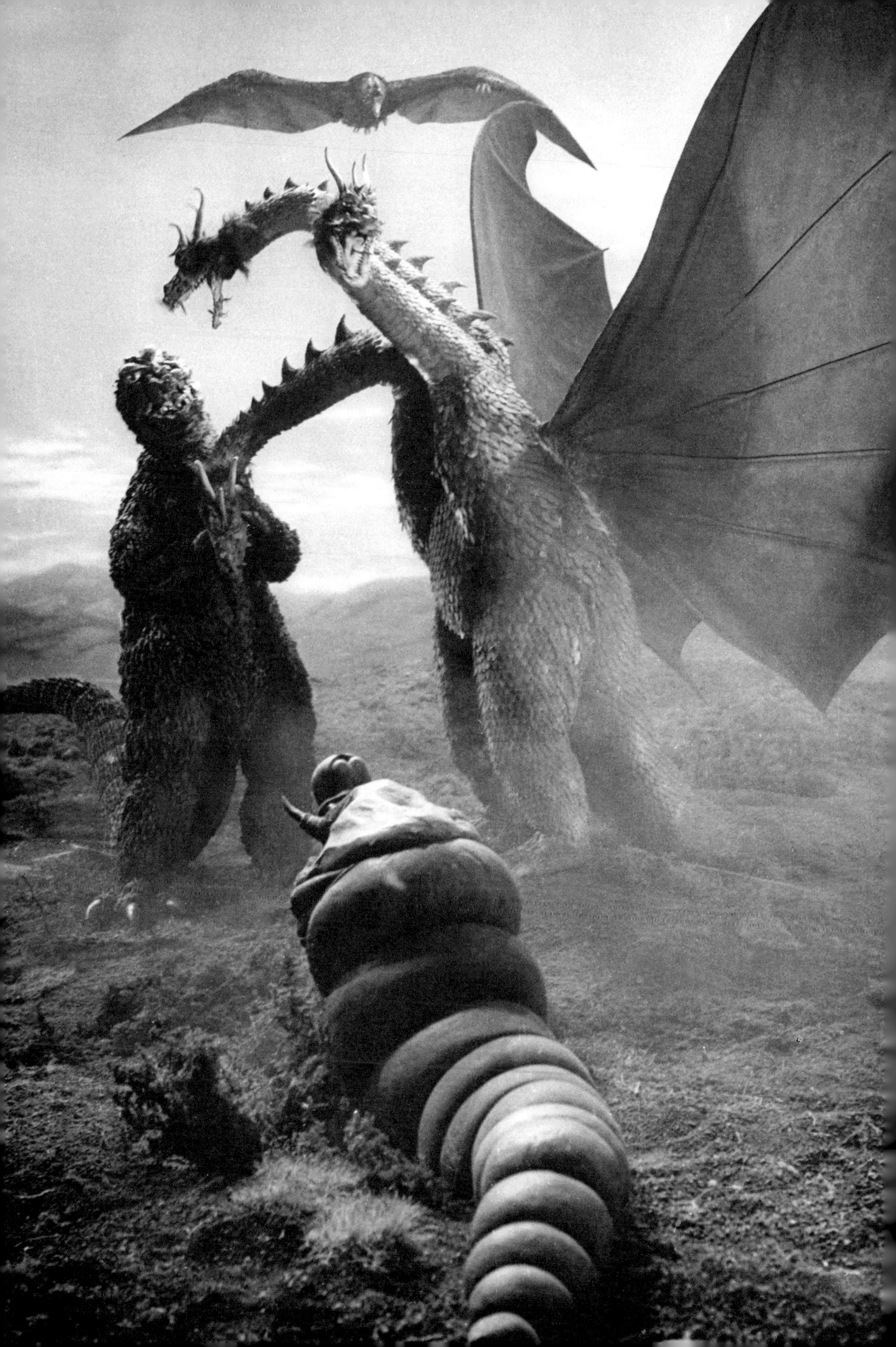

Godzilla Series filmography

	1.	*Godzilla*	1954	Godzilla
Showa Series	2.	*Godzilla Raids Again*	1955	Godzilla, Anguirus
	3.	*King Kong vs. Godzilla*	1962	Godzilla, King Kong, Giant Octopus, Giant Lizard
	4.	*Mothra vs. Godzilla*	1964	Godzilla, Mothra (two larvae), Mothra (imago)
	5.	*Ghidorah, the Three-Headed Monster*	1964	Rodan, Godzilla, Mothra (larva), King Ghidorah
	6.	*Invasion of Astro-Monster*	1965	Rodan, Godzilla, King Ghidorah
	7.	*Ebirah, Horror of the Deep*	1966	Godzilla, Ebirah, Mothra (imago), Giant Condor
	8.	*Son of Godzilla*	1967	Godzilla, Minilla, Kamacuras, Kumonga
	9.	*Destroy All Monsters*	1968	Rodan, Godzilla, Minilla, Mothra (larva), Anguirus, Baragon, Gorosaurus, Manda, Varan, Kumonga, King Ghidorah
	10.	*All Monsters Attack*	1969	Godzilla, Minilla, Gabara, Kamacuras
	11.	*Godzilla vs. Hedorah*	1971	Godzilla, Hedorah
	12.	*Godzilla vs. Gigan*	1972	Godzilla, Anguirus, King Ghidorah, Gigan
	13.	*Godzilla vs. Megalon*	1973	Godzilla, Megalon, Jet Jaguar, Gigan, Anguirus
	14.	*Godzilla vs. Mechagodzilla*	1974	Godzilla, Anguirus, Mechagodzilla, King Caesar
	15.	*Terror of Mechagodzilla*	1975	Godzilla, Mechagodzilla II, Titanosaurus
Heisei Series	16.	*The Return of Godzilla*	1984	Godzilla
	17.	*Godzilla vs. Biollante*	1989	Godzilla, Biollante
	18.	*Godzilla vs. King Ghidorah*	1991	Godzillasaurus/Godzilla, Dorat/King Ghidorah
	19.	*Godzilla vs. Mothra*	1992	Godzilla, Mothra (larva/imago), Battra (larva/imago)
	20.	*Godzilla vs. Mechagodzilla 2*	1993	Rodan, Godzilla, Mechagodzilla
	21.	*Godzilla vs. SpaceGodzilla*	1994	Godzilla, Little Godzilla, SpaceGodzilla, Moguera, Fairy Mothra
	22.	*Godzilla vs. Destoroyah*	1995	Godzilla, Godzilla Jr., Destoroyah
Millennium Series	23.	*Godzilla 2000: Millennium*	1999	Godzilla, Millennian/Orga
	24.	*Godzilla vs. Megaguirus*	2000	Godzilla, Maganulon/Maganula, Giant Maganulon/Megaguirus
	25.	*Godzilla, Mothra and King Ghidorah: Giant Monsters All-Out Attack*	2001	Godzilla, Mothra (larva/imago), King Ghidorah, Baragon
	26.	*Godzilla Against Mechagodzilla*	2002	Godzilla, Mechagodzilla
	27.	*Godzilla: Tokyo SOS*	2003	Godzilla, Mechagodzilla, Mothra (imago), Mothra (two larvae), Kamoebas
	28.	*Godzilla Final Wars*	2004	Godzilla, Minilla, Mothra (imago), Kamacuras, Kumonga, Gigan, Manda, Ebirah, Anguirus, King Caesar, Hedorah

Godzilla, King Ghidorah, and Mothra spar in a three-way battle in *Ghidorah, the Three-Headed Monster*.

Close-up view of the bronze Godzilla statue in front of the Toho Chanter Cinema, just beside the head offices of Toho near Tokyo's Hibiya park. A plaque on the sculpture's base reads, "Don't think this is the last Godzilla" (November 8th, 1954). This ominous warning is ascribed to paleontologist Dr. Kyohei Yamane, the character of the professor from the original Godzilla film. **Following spread:** In *Godzilla* (1954), the title character makes his way through Tokyo Bay to launch his first assault on the city.

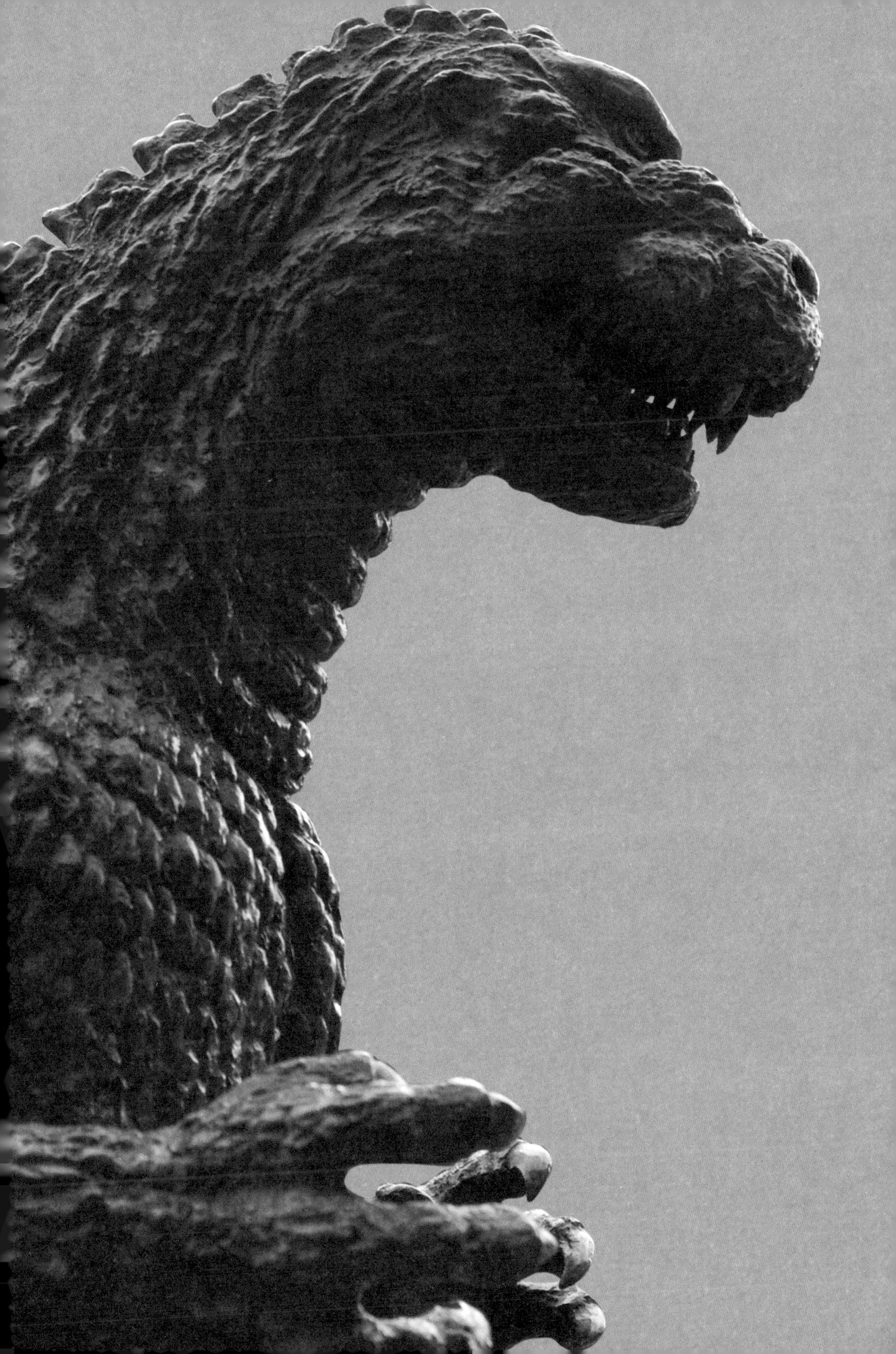

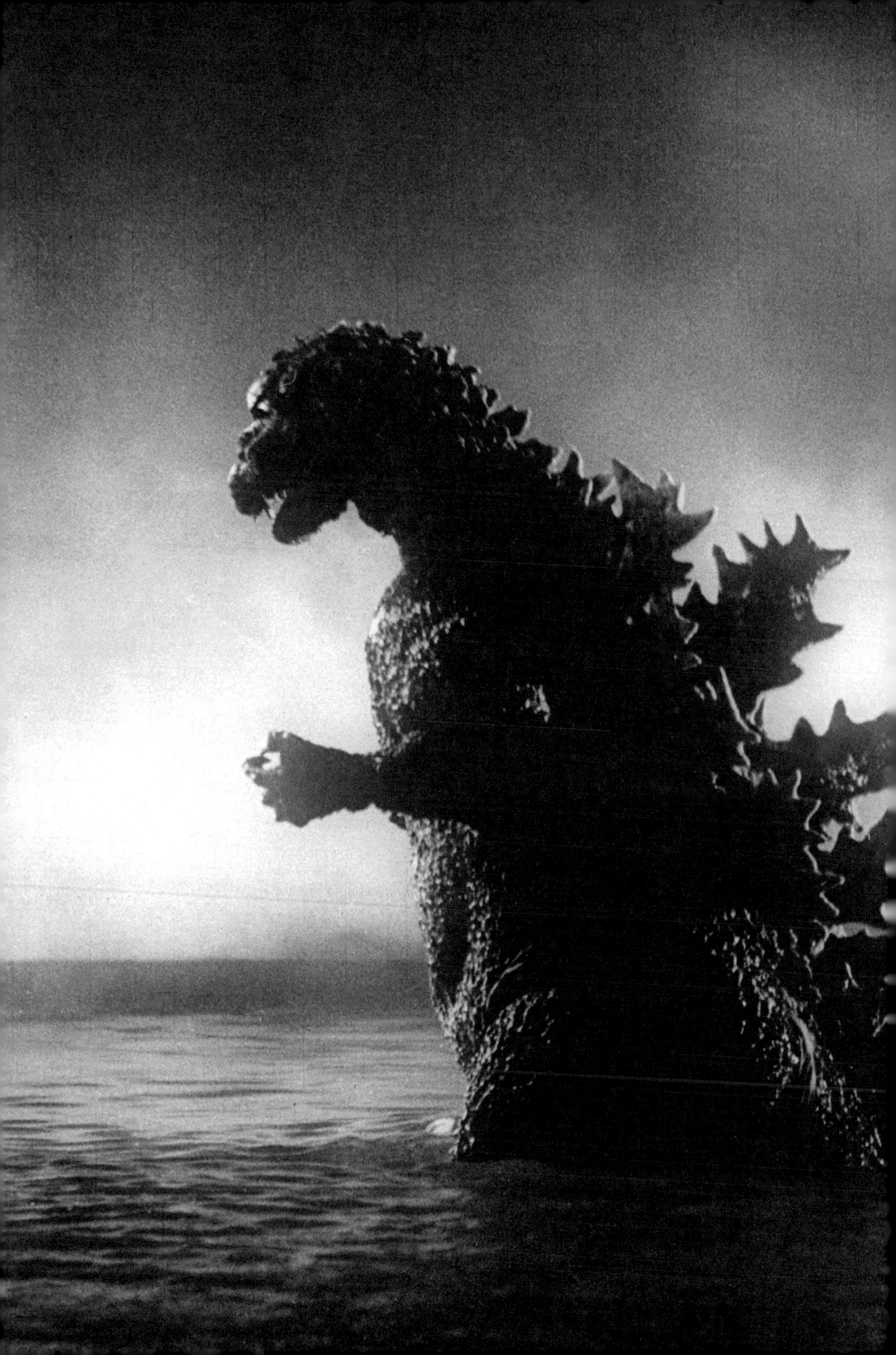

Following spread: In the 1954 Godzilla film, the title monster lays waste to the Ginza area in Tokyo. The Matsuzakaya building, which is readily identifiable as one of the structures that is destroyed, issued a formal complaint to the movie's producers. They claimed the scene of their building on fire was a bad omen. Since that time, destruction of a model based on an actual building requires the permission of the property's owner. In an interesting twist, the sales revenue of the department store increased considerably thanks to the attention it received in the film, thus prompting a number of building owners to beseech film producers to have models of their buildings destroyed in kaiju films.

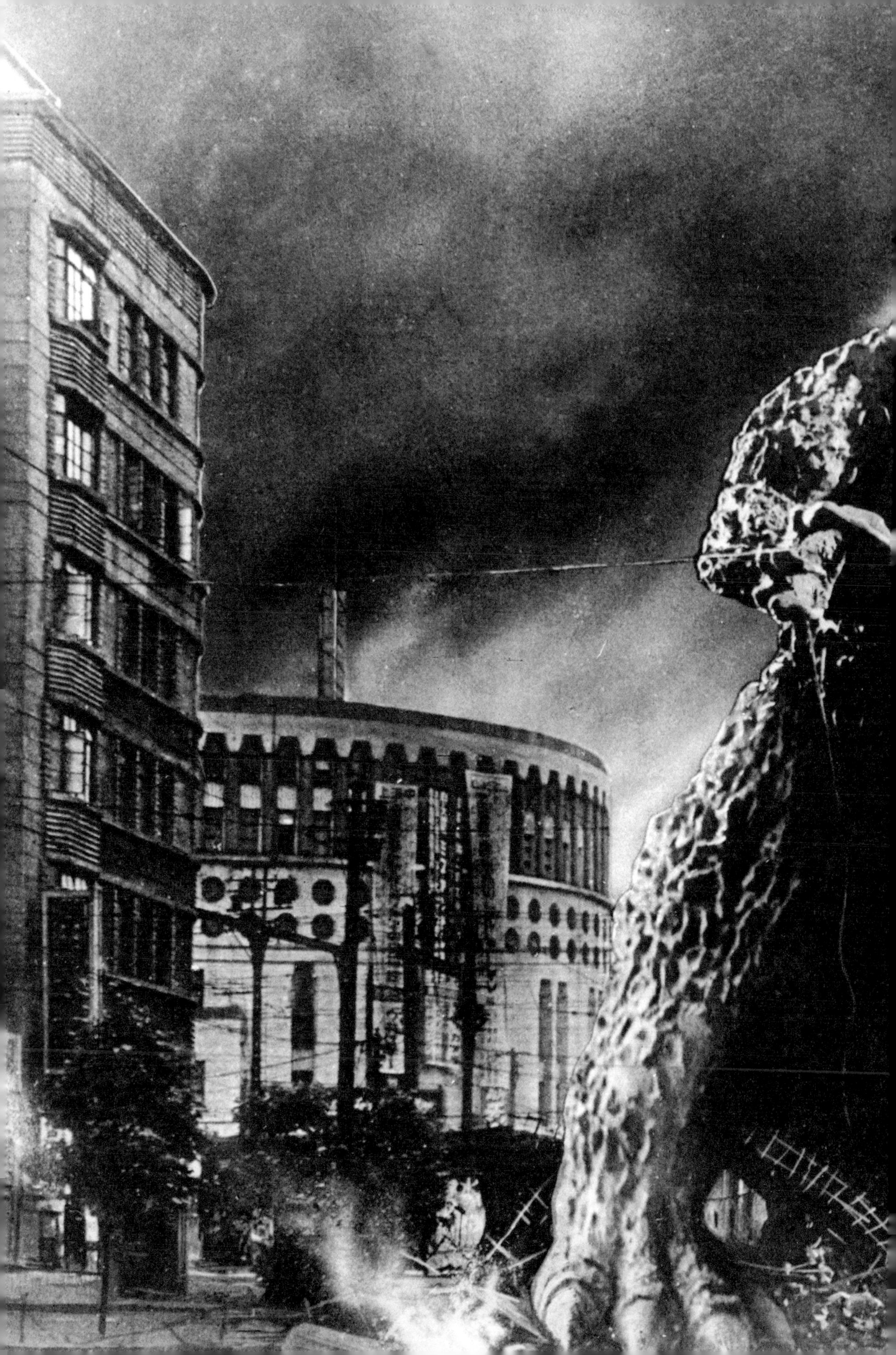

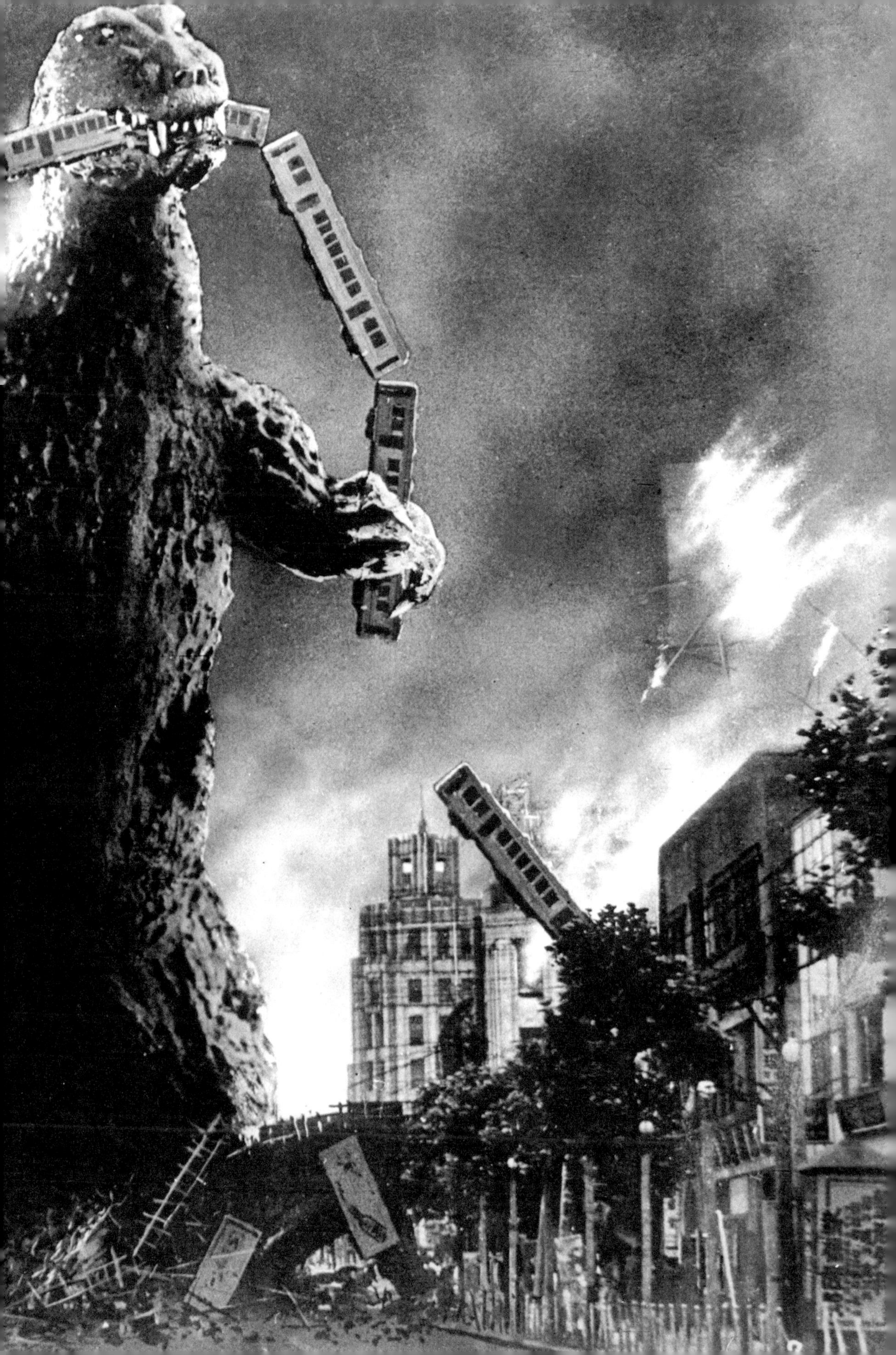

A scene from *Godzilla: Tokyo SOS* (2003). Tokyo is still the object of the monster's tormenting in this film, the twenty-seventh in the series.

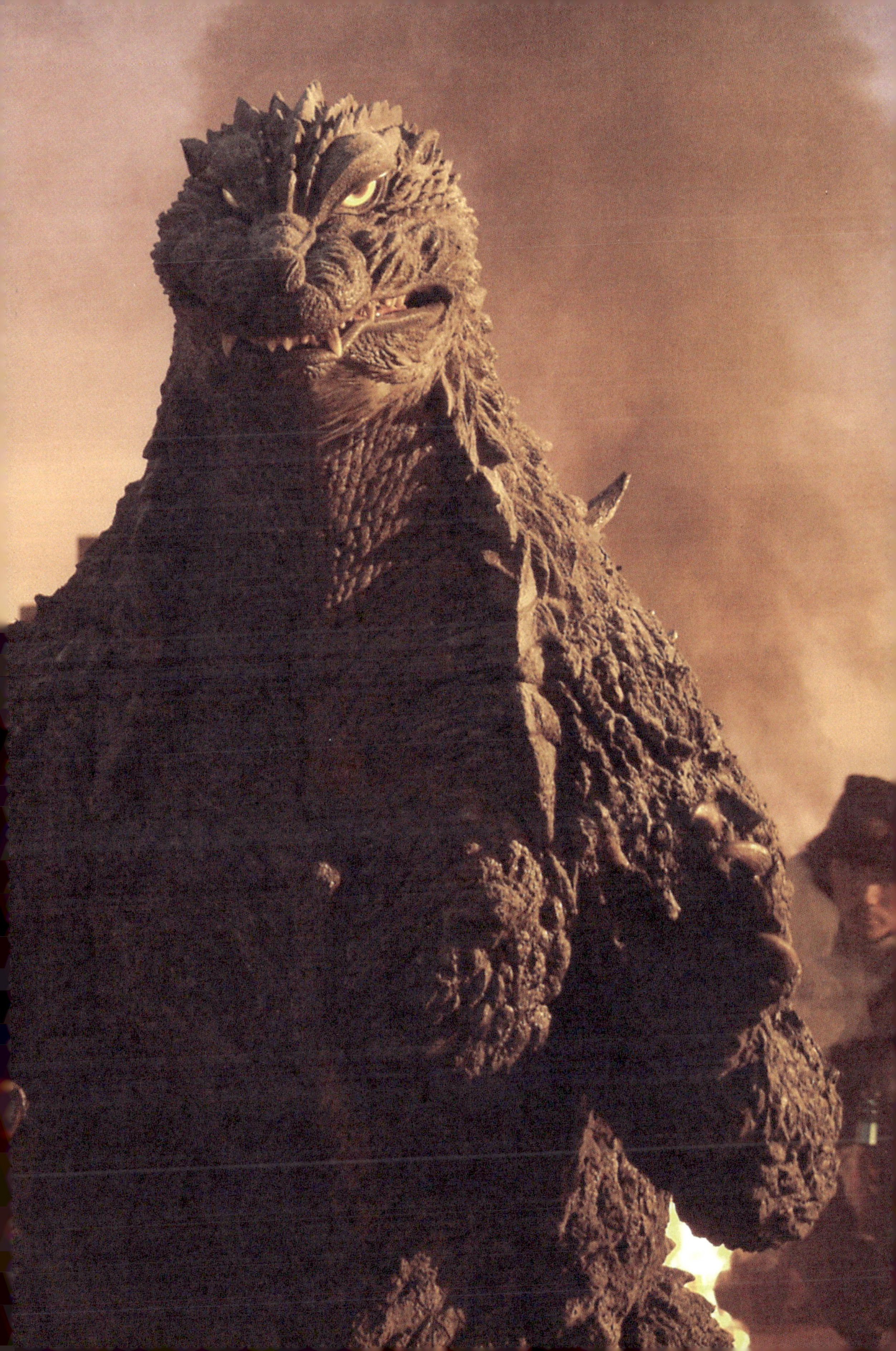

アンギラス
Anguirus

In 1955, some six months after the release of the original Godzilla film, *Godzilla Raids Again* was released as the second film in the series and featured Anguirus. This was the first kaiju-versus-kaiju battle in the series. Like Godzilla, Anguirus is a dinosaur that is reanimated as a consequence of nuclear testing. Godzilla and Anguirus both existed at the same time in prehistory: the Triassic period, 150 million years ago. Anguirus is thought to be a descendent of the Ankylosaurus dinosaur, which had extensive armor covering its entire dorsal length and had a long, clublike tail. These features were incorporated into the character design of Anguirus. The head design was by Teizou Toshimitu (1909–1982), who from 1954 was principally involved in the design of special effects at Toho and often collaborated with the brother duo of Kanju and Yasuei Yagi, who were responsible for the kaiju torsos. Eizo Kaimai made the spikes on its back.

Anguirus's mental facilities are dispersed throughout its body, giving it great agility in battle. The first-generation Anguirus loathes any kaiju apart from its own species and has a ferocious character. After battling Godzilla at the mythical Iwato Island, the fight continued in Osaka. Though Anguirus's upright height is greater than that of Godzilla, it is burned to death by Godzilla's heat beam. As Anguirus lies dying it lets out a wail of such a magnitude that it cracks the stone walls of Osaka Castle. In the original story, the creature is able to spit the same heat beam as Godzilla, but in the film it has no such faculty. In the original design of the character the dorsal shell was divided in two plates. The two plates were melded into one contiguous plate to help the movement of the actor wearing the suit. The facial expressions of the creature are for the most part operated with one hand by this actor. The spikes on the plate were metal, covered with *washi* (Japanese paper), and colored a bright emerald green—though this is lost in the black-and-white film. According to press releases that accompanied the original release of the movie, Anguirus is from Siberia. The second generation of Anguirus (as seen in *Destroy All Monsters*) has a warm and devoted character and its screech is slightly different. So much for holding a grudge.

Filmography
1. *Godzilla Raids Again* (1955)
2. *Destroy All Monsters* (1968)
3. *Godzilla vs. Gigan* (1972)
4. *Godzilla vs. Megalon* (1973)
5. *Godzilla vs. Mechagodzilla* (1974)
6. *Godzilla Final Wars* (2004)

Anguirus in *Godzilla Raids Again* (1955)

Production Company: Toho | **STATS Height:** Up to 160m **Weight:** Up to 60,000 tons **Flight speed:** N/A **Origin:** Seatopia | **Powers:** Reverse impale attack / massive leaps / underground burrowing

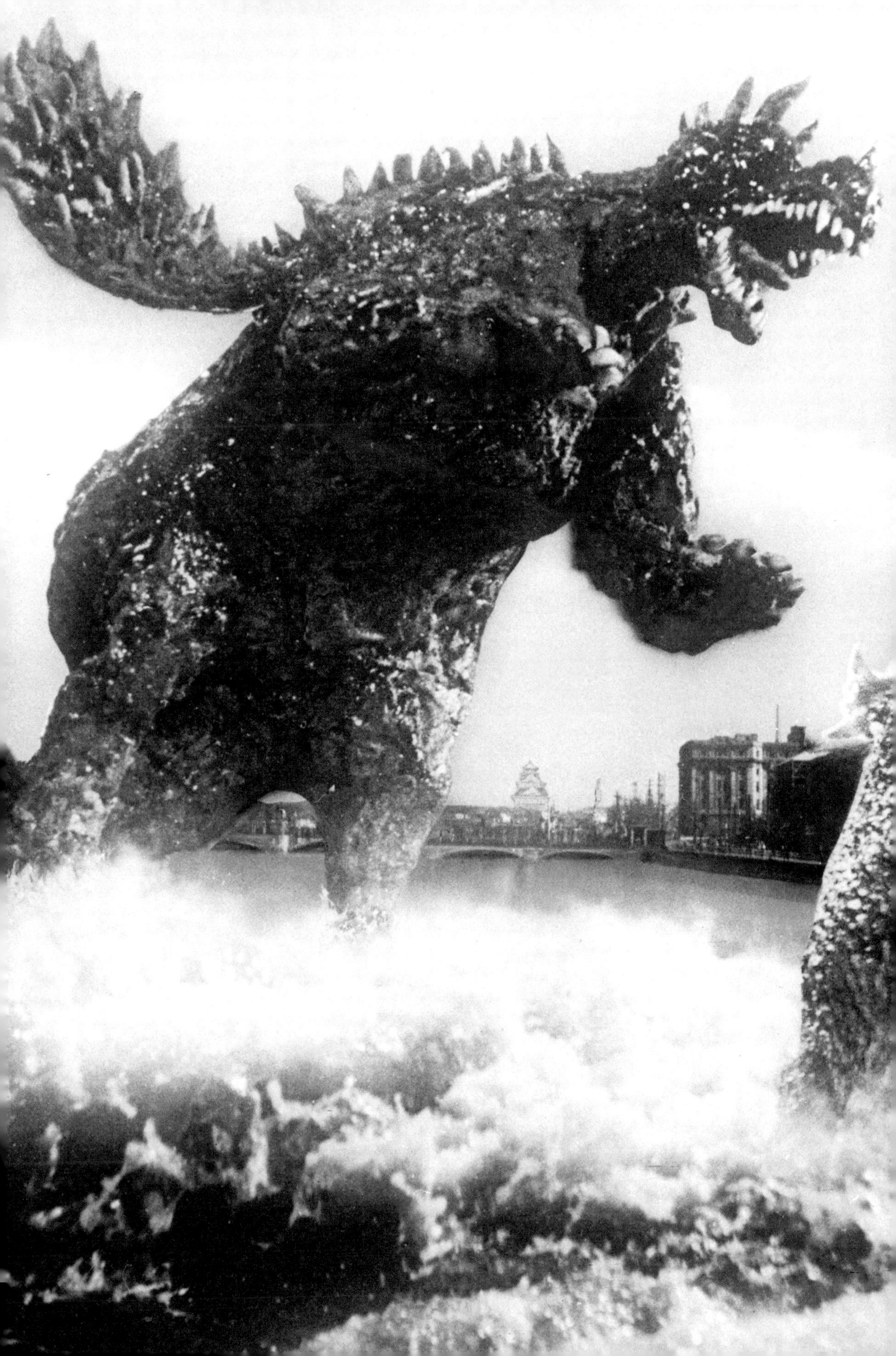

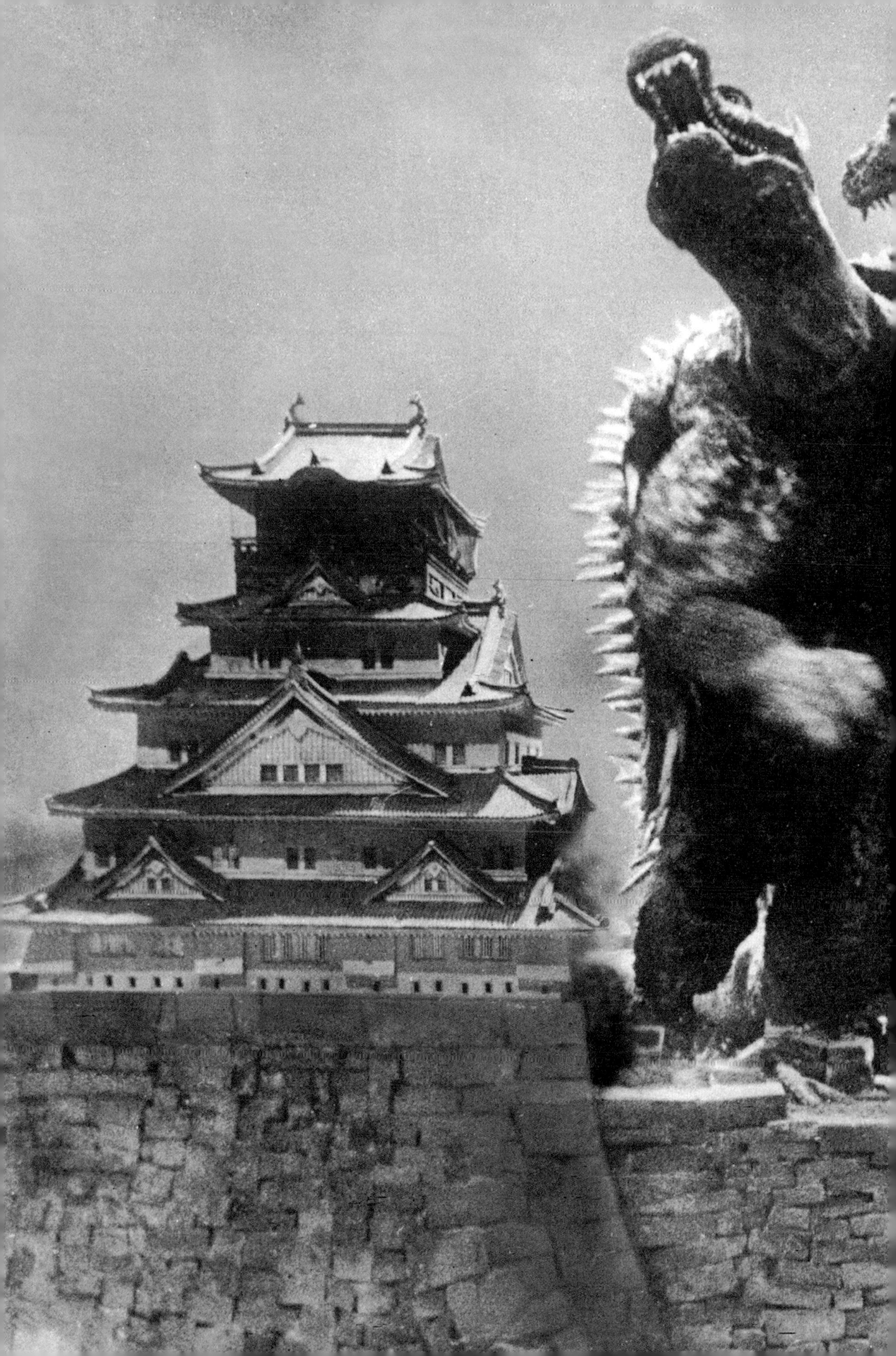

The battle between Godzilla and Anguirus reaches its climax at Osaka Castle, where Anguirus is vanquished.

モスラ
Mothra

The film *Mothra* was released in 1961 as part of the series of kaiju films produced by Toho. It was the first kaiju film released in the wide-screen format. The character has appeared in thirteen film productions, including one remake in 1996 which had little to do with the original story. While in the first film Mothra does not battle other kaiju, in the second (*Mothra vs. Godzilla*) and subsequent films the character is always engaged in battle—several times with Godzilla. Mothra is a kaiju along with Godzilla and Rodan that Toho actively developed.

Released in the year after the 1960 peace accord, the first Mothra film was planned for simultaneous worldwide release. Rorishika (an anagram of Russia and America in Japanese) was a thinly veiled surrogate for America, whose military presence in Japan at the time was palpable. So it is no accident that Mothra passes through the American Yokota Air Base in Tokyo. Other political circumstances in Japan at the time were obvious subtexts in the film. Pamphlets about feminist issues or printed matter related to aboriginal race relations were pinned up on walls in certain scenes.

In the original *Godzilla*, an elder tells of the rituals meant to appease the monster. Similarly, *Mothra* introduces a tribal theme, which has the monster and tribe people in a system of cohabitation. Somewhere in the Pacific there is a jungle island called Infant Island. A country called Rorishika is carrying out hydrogen bomb tests there. The tribal inhabitants are a peaceful people who pray to their guardian deity Mothra. The primitive people of the island are protected by the two tiny *bishojo* (beautiful young girls). They reveal themselves to a team of researchers on the island and divulge the existence of the tribe and their god. These two characters were originally played by singing duo The Peanuts (twins Emi and Yuri Ito). They sing the Mothra song, which is based on Bahasa Indonesian. (The song is a plea for the divine protection of Mothra and a prayer for peace.) Their unison singing can awaken Mothra from its state of gestation. The duo makes appearances in other films in the series and plays a critical role in advancing the plot and at times, they serve as interpreters for the kaiju. In *Ghidorah, the Three-Headed Monster* for instance, they provide an intelligible explanation of the protracted debate among Mothra, Godzilla, and Rodan about whether they should team up to fight King Ghidorah.

Filmography

1. *Mothra* (1961) 2. *Mothra vs. Godzilla* (1961) 3. *Ghidorah, the Three-Headed Monster* (1964) 4. *All Monsters Attack* (1966) 5. *Destroy All Monsters* (1968) 6. *Godzilla vs. Mothra* (1992) 7. *Godzilla vs. SpaceGodzilla* (1994) 8. *Mothra* (1996) 9. *Rebirth of Mothra II* (1997) 10. *Rebirth of Mothra III* (1998) 11. *Godzilla, Mothra and King Ghidorah: Giant Monsters All-Out Attack* (2001) 12. *Godzilla: Tokyo SOS* (2003)

Original movie poster for *Mothra vs. Godzilla* (1961)

Production Company: Toho | **STATS Height:** 120m as larva; 65m as imago **Weight:** Up to 16,500 tons as larva; Up to 22,000 tons as imago / **Flight speed:** Mach 80 **Origin:** Egg hatched on Infant Island | **Powers:** Yellow poison powder / silk thread trap (larva) / hurricane and lightning / energy beams

東宝
マッハ3の巨蛾か！ミサイル重戦車のゴジラか！空・海・陸を揺がす世紀の激斗
総天然色
モスラ対ゴジラ
GODZILLA AGAINST MOTHRA
監督 本多猪四郎
特技監督 円谷英二
製作 田中友幸
脚本 関沢新一
宝田明
星由里子
ザ・ピーナッツ
小泉博
藤木悠
佐原健二
田島義文
小杉義男
藤田進
田崎潤

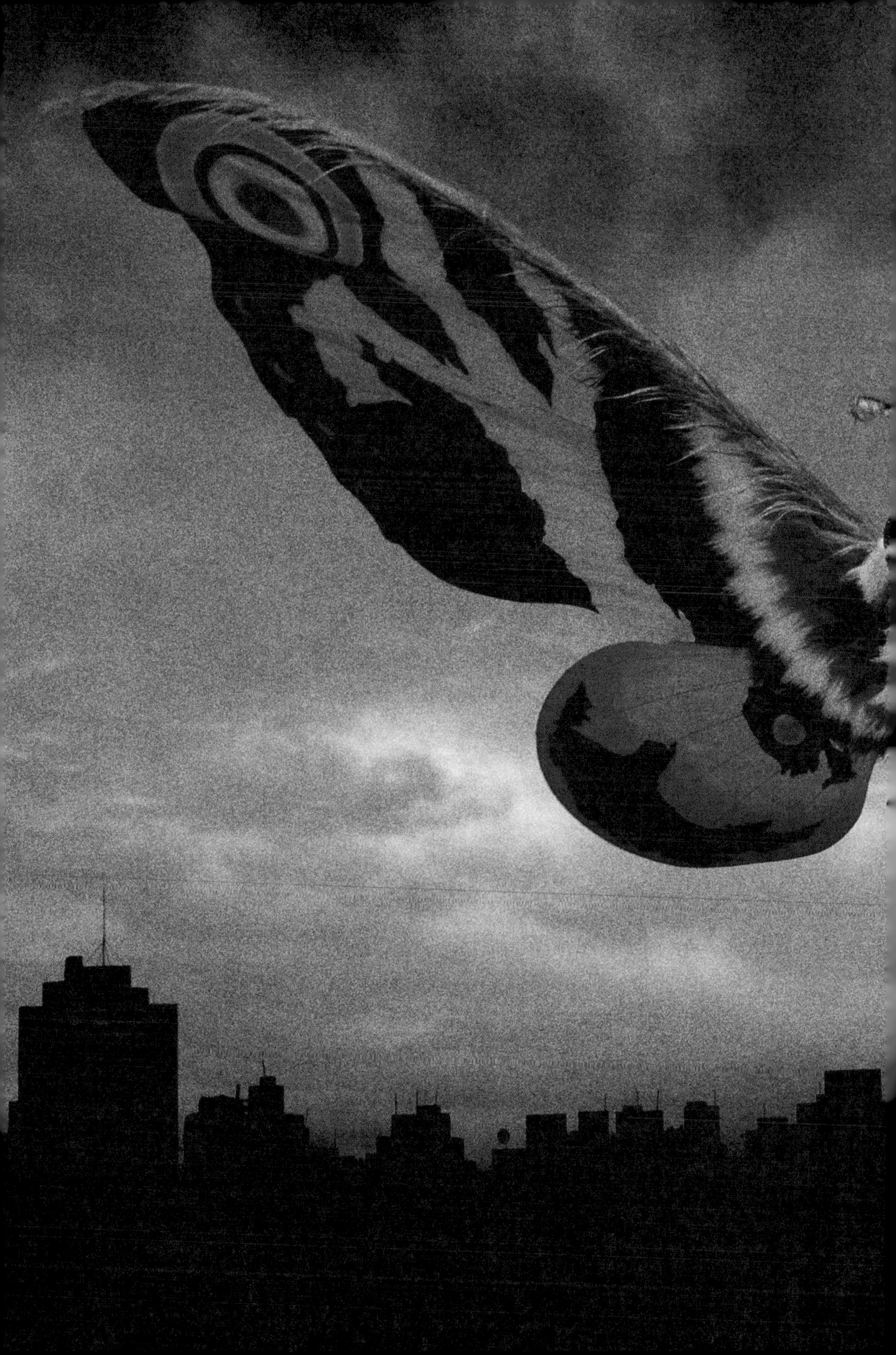

In *Godzilla Final Wars* (2004), the last installment of the series, each of the most popular kaiju characters makes an appearance in a showdown-style battle of the greats.

Godzilla's and Mothra's relationship is one fraught with tension. Their first meeting was in battle, as shown here in a scene from *Mothra vs. Godzilla* (1964). Later on they find themselves joining forces to battle other, more menacing kaiju who have come to visit destruction upon Tokyo.

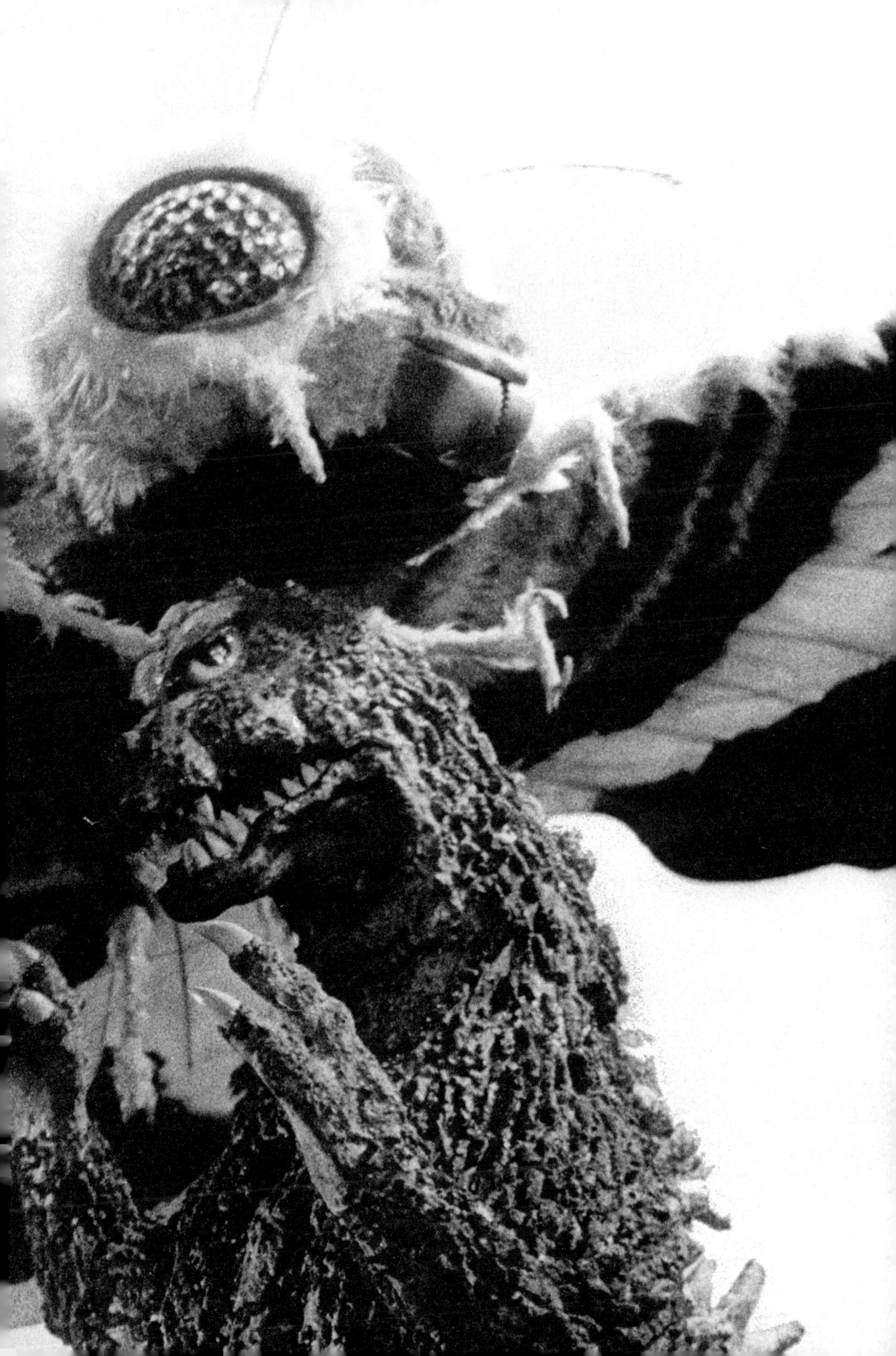

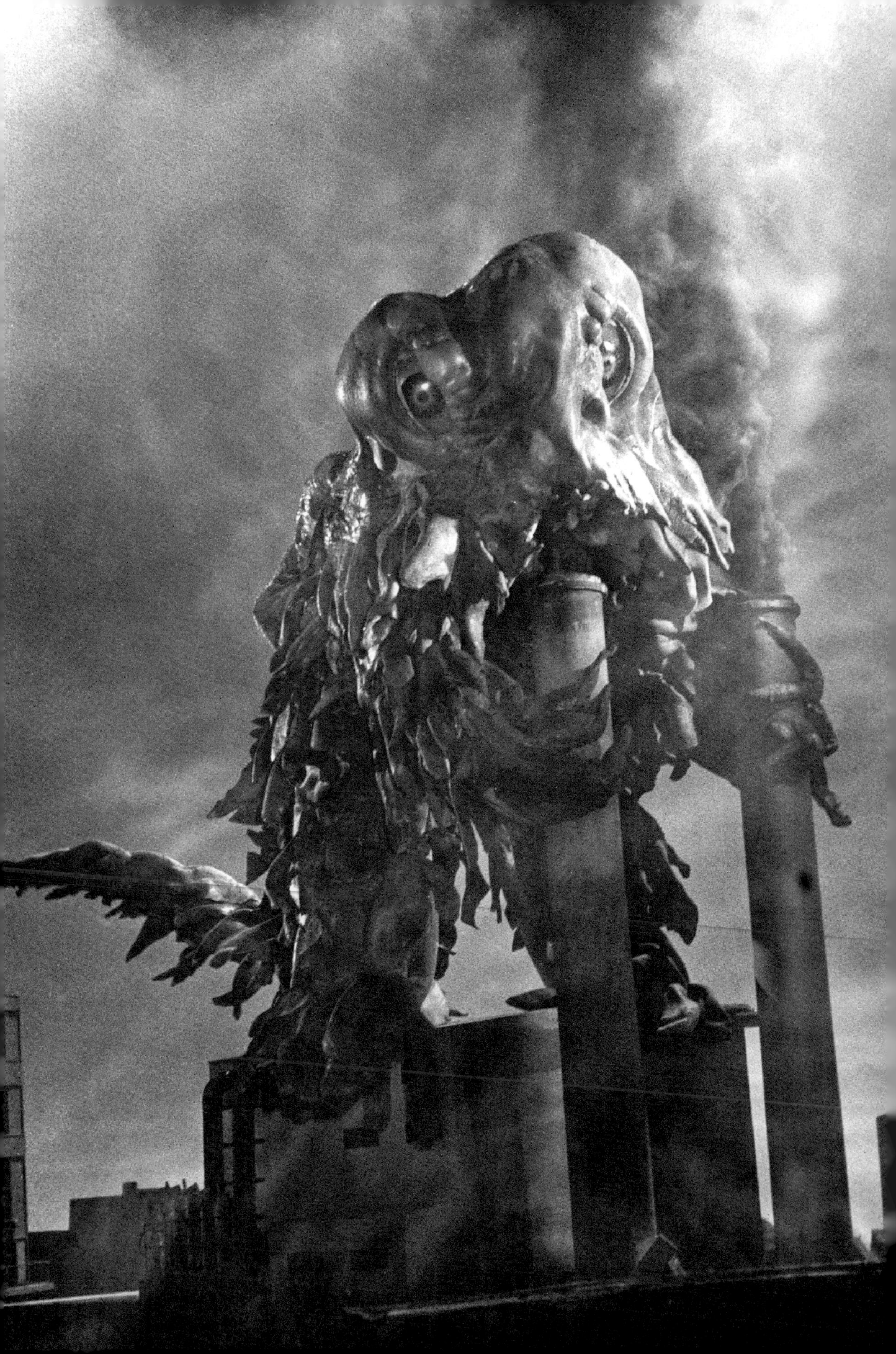

ヘドラ
Hedorah

Hedorah when on dry land in Godzilla vs. Hedorah (1971).

Godzilla vs. Hedorah was released in 1971 as the eleventh in the Godzilla series. Several of the films incorporated contemporary social issues in the narrative's backdrop. In this film, introducing Hedorah, pollution was the principal issue. Even though the character has the air of a space alien, Hedorah is a byproduct of contaminated ocean water in the vicinity. This particular topic was in wide discussion at the time. There was a great deal of public awareness of the pollution of sediment—known in Japanese as "Hedoro"—in the Port of Tagonoura, located in the southern part of Japan's main island. The paper manufacturing industry was booming at the time and this resulted in pollution of the coastal waters. In the 1960s, hazardous waste issues plagued many manufacturing towns that were lacking in regulatory standards and goaded by pressures to compete in industry. One notable tragic result is Minamata Disease (a neurological syndrome caused by mercury poisoning), which was documented by W. Eugene Smith in the 1970s. In 1971, there was an incident where a group of schoolgirls were rendered unconscious on a school playground by exposure to a photochemical smog. This was the inspiration for director Sakano to make this film and gave Hedorah's rampage in the movie an element of realism. Previous films in the series were geared toward children. This film presented its audience with darker themes, including many scenes of violence—a tone reflected in the soundtrack. The film, nonetheless, steers clear of being didactic and delivers an entertaining battle with Godzilla, who is a hero of the human race in this feature.

Hedorah's body morphs depending on its level of water saturation. Once it absorbs water its individual fragments take on the form of tadpoles, which then recombine to make an even bigger figure. As it dries, it develops legs for terrestrial locomotion. These appendages continue to develop and eventually give Hedorah the power of flight and the ability to shoot rays of light. This kaiju has a store of nuclear power that provides energy for these functions. While in flight mode, Hedorah picks up and carries Godzilla, throws him into an opening in the side of a mountain, and sprays him with contaminated silt. The mist of sulfuric acid that Hedorah releases can rust metal and strip flesh from bone. He crushes one of Godzilla's eyes and reduces one of his arms to bone. When completely dry, Hedorah is very difficult to beat. For some fans, it is the most formidable of kaiju.

Filmography
1. *Godzilla vs. Hedorah* (1971)
2. *Godzilla Final Wars* (2004)

Production Company: Toho | **STATS Height:** Up to 120m | **Weight:** Up to 70,000 tons | **Flight speed:** Mach 1 | **Origin:** Irradiated Godzillasaurus from Sogell Island |
Powers: Deadly smog / Acidic slime / Sulphuric acid mist / Self-regeneration

Emerging from the highly contaminated sludge that created it, Hedorah moves toward land. This kaiju changes shape depending on its exposure to water. Here its form resembles that of a tadpole, but once on land it develops appendages that function as arms and legs. **Following spread:** A scene from *Godzilla vs. Hedorah* (1971). **Pages 48–49:** Hedorah and Godzilla do battle.

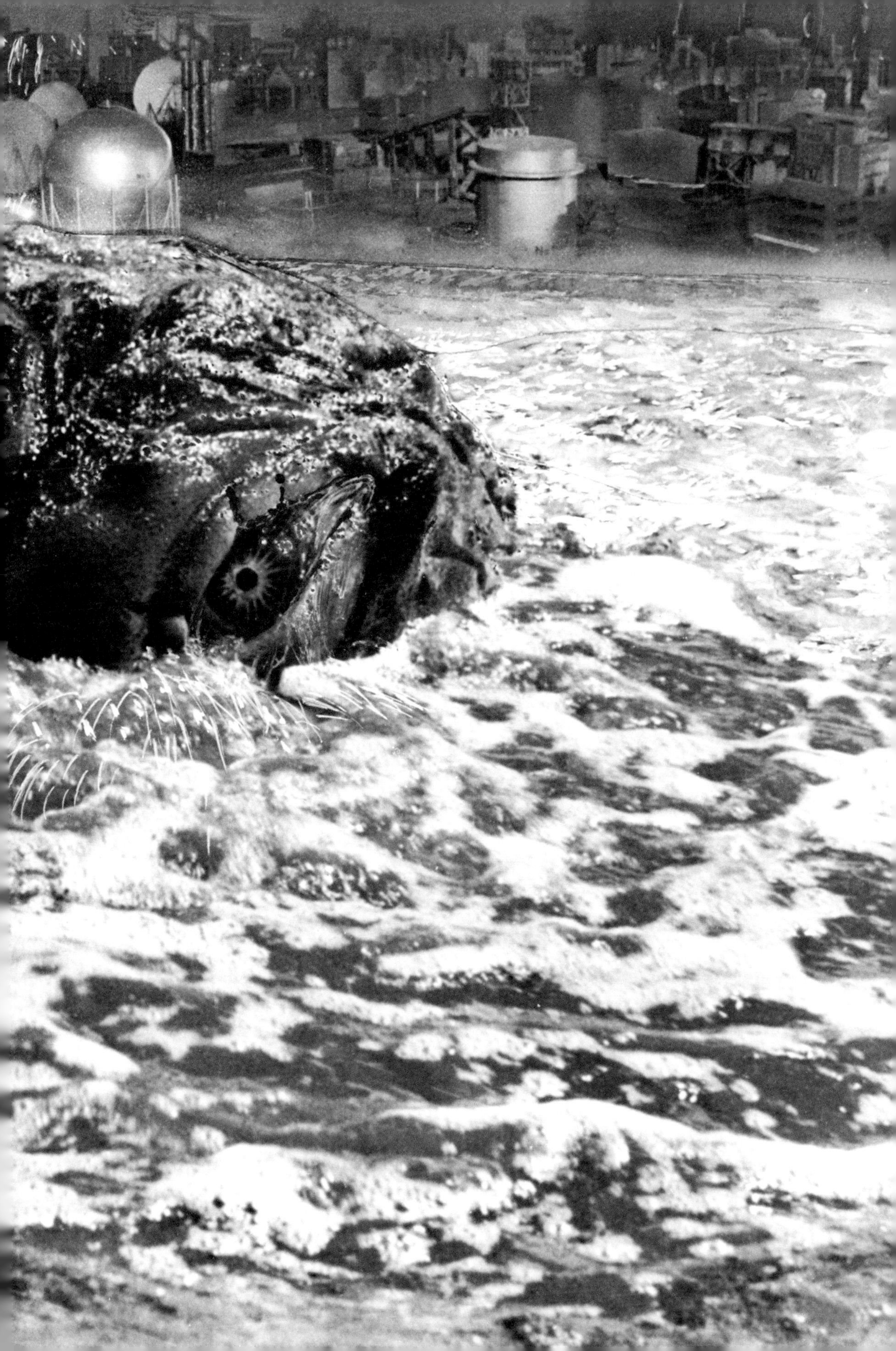

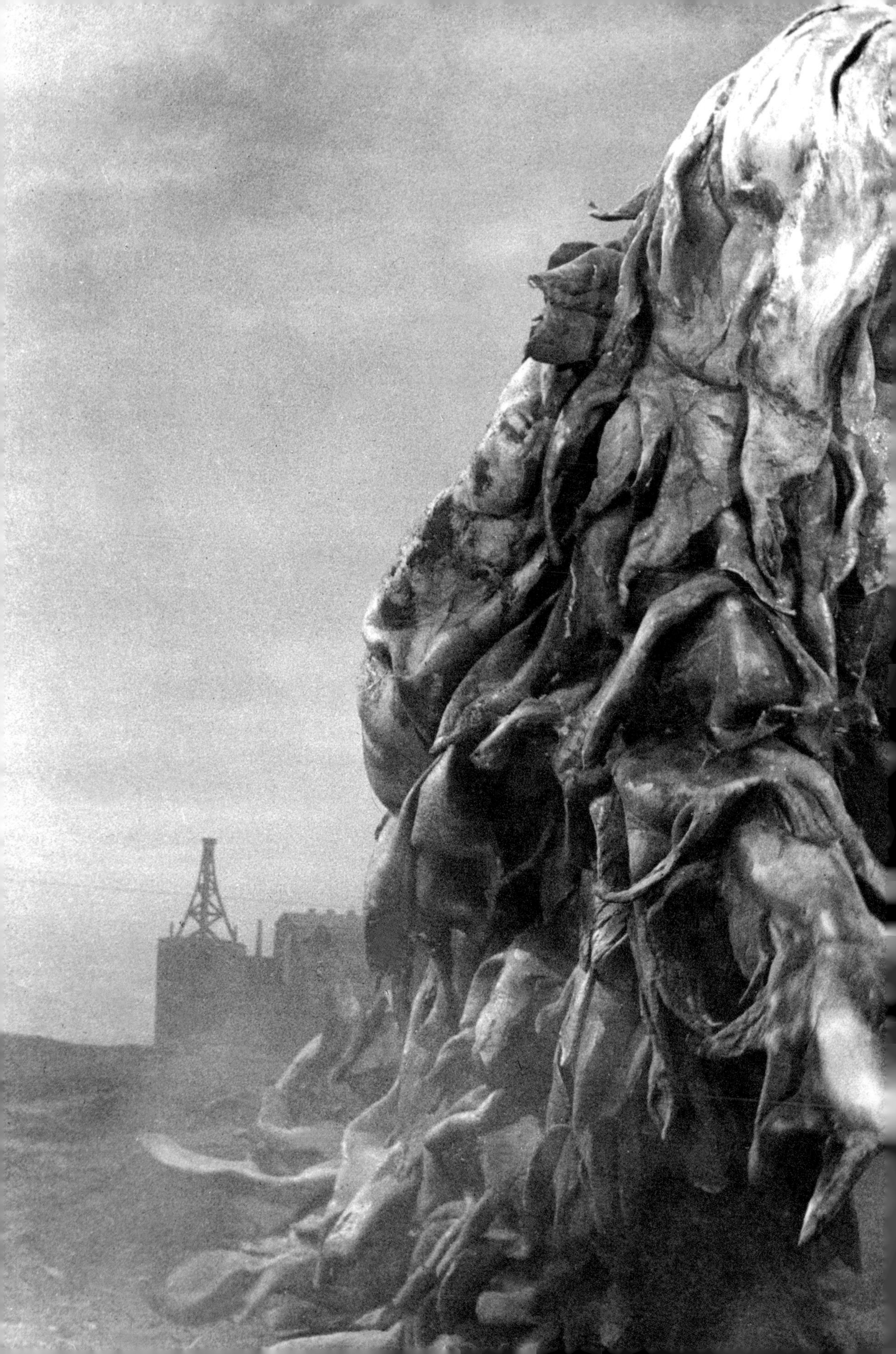

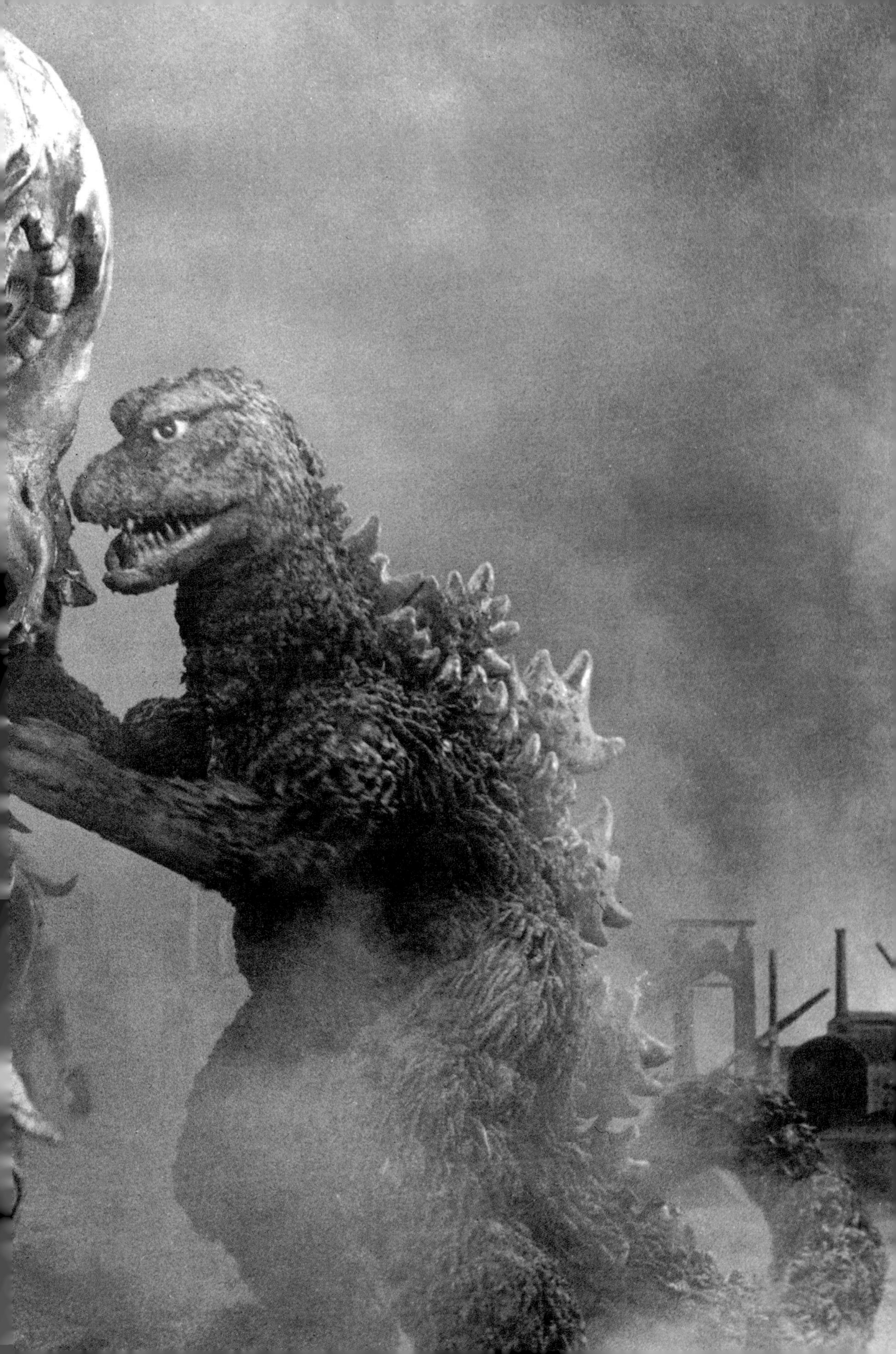

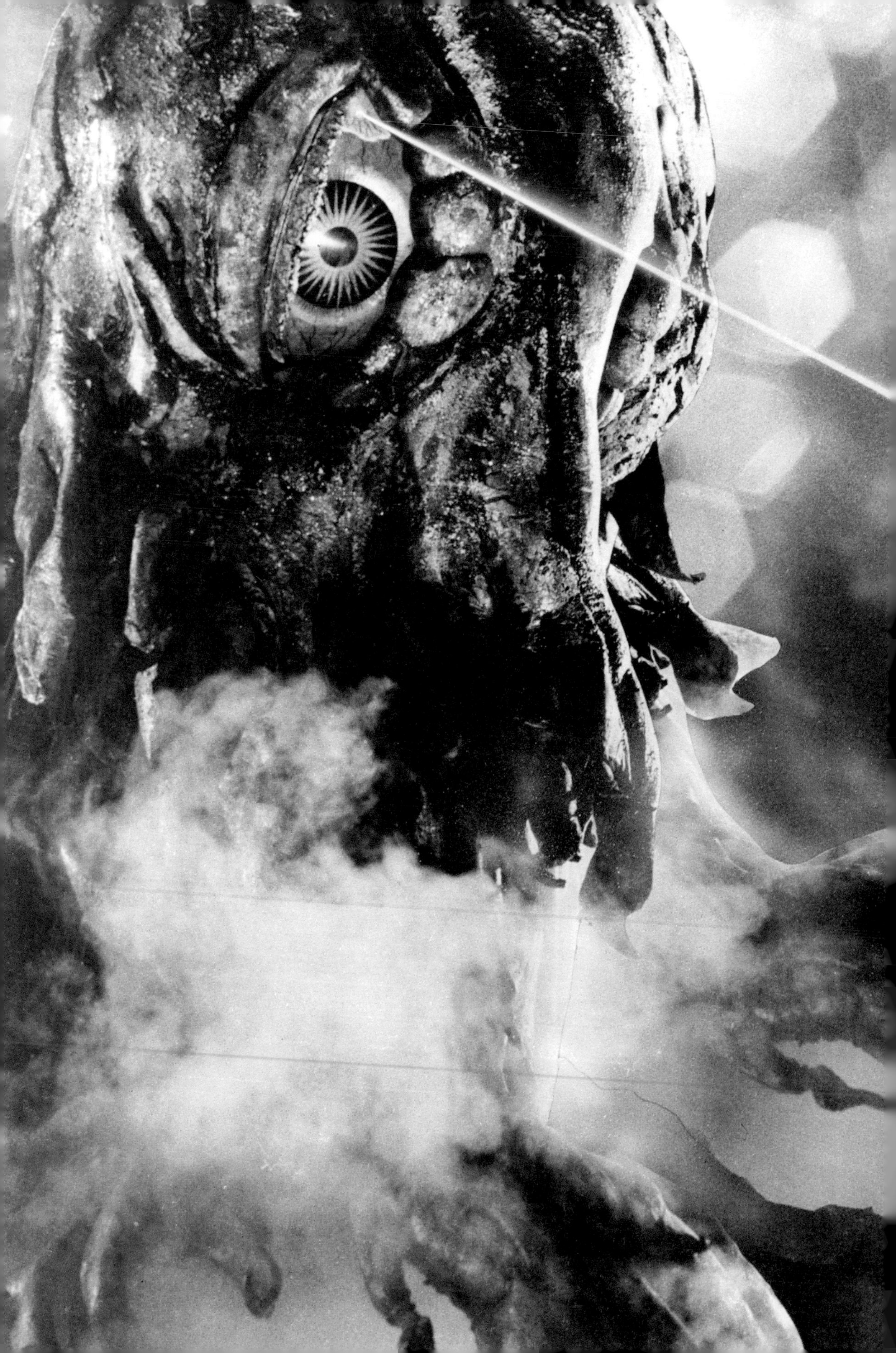

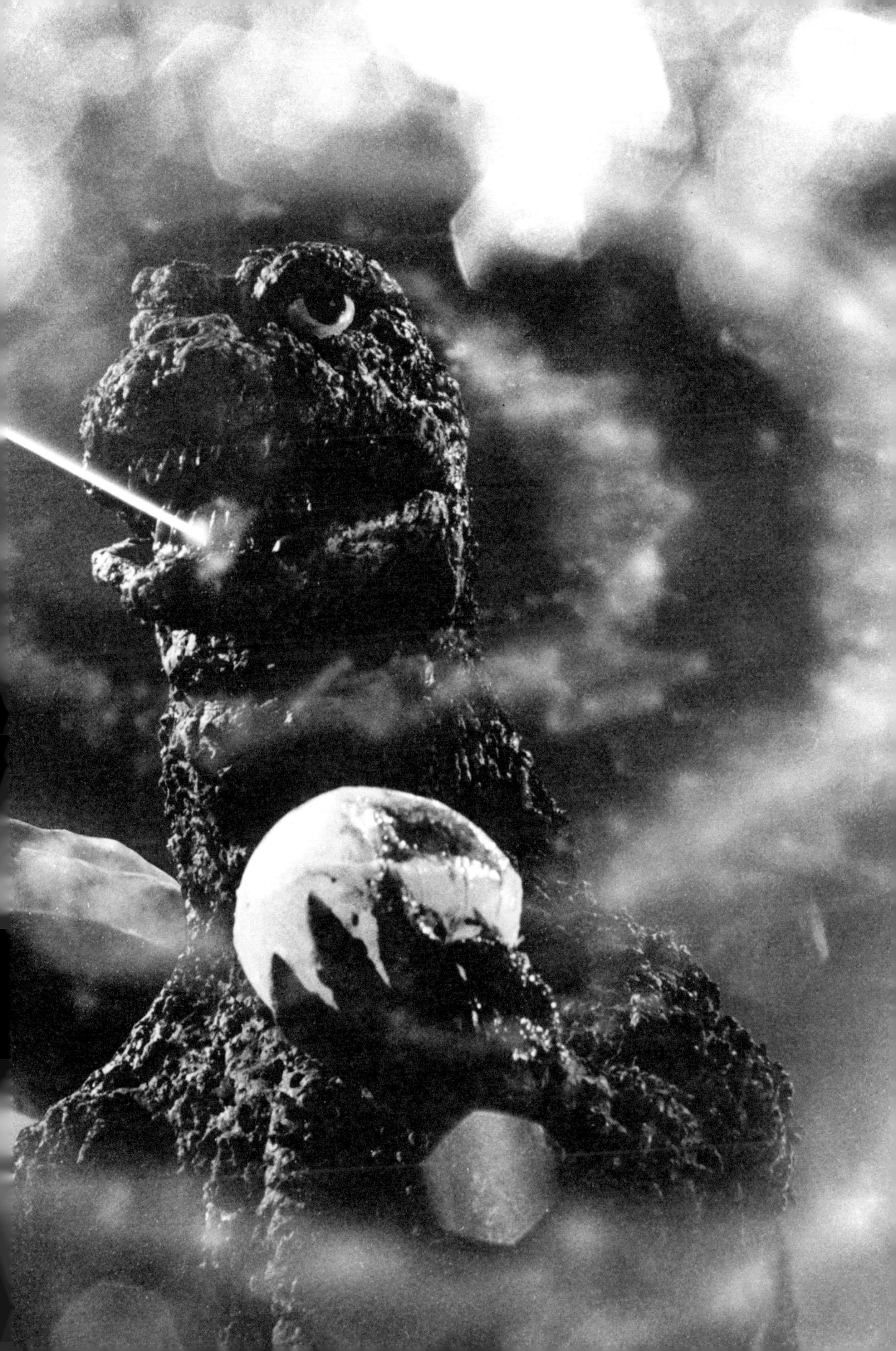

キングギドラ
King Ghidorah

Since making its first appearance in the 1964 Toho film *Ghidorah, the Three-Headed Monster* (in which this character battled Godzilla, Mothra, and Rodan), King Ghidorah has gone on to do battle and wreak havoc in several other Toho films. With crescent-shaped horns atop its three foreheads, three long necks, two long tails, gold-colored scales, and a pair of giant wings (instead of arms), King Ghidorah certainly has a majestic presence. From its mouth spits magnetic ray-like bolts of lightning. King Ghidorah's image is based on a 1959 Toho special effects film about Japanese mythology called *Nihon Tanjo* ("Origin of Japan"), which included the figure of *Yamata Orochi*, a gigantic serpent with eight heads. Ilja Muromets, a 1959 Soviet film featuring a fire-spitting three-headed dragon, was also an inspiration for King Ghidorah. The original design was by Akira Watanabe with the head sculpted by Teizou Toshimitu and the torso made by the Yagi brothers. The initial designs were made to look more like a dragon, as directed by Eiji Tsuburaya, and the head was made to look like the guardian sculptures found at Shinto shrines. Even though the King Ghidorah costume is a suit like Godzilla, with its three heads, large wing span, and two tails in back, approximately twenty-five crew members were needed to move the different parts of the figure independently using piano wires. The ability to carry out such feats of extreme difficulty in figure operation represents the golden era of Toho's kaiju filmmaking.

In almost all productions King Ghidorah's role is evil or that of the enemy, and it is the kaiju that has battled on screen with Godzilla most often. Among Godzilla fans it is considered Godzilla's greatest rival (or the strongest enemy) in the entire series. King Ghidorah has a cyborg incarnation called Mecha King Ghidorah, a subspecies kaiju Death Ghidorah, Kaizah Ghidorah, and other variations. Gigan also has wings similar to King Ghidorah and golden scales, leading to speculation about genealogical connections between the space kaiju Gigan and the Ghidorah tribe. Even though King Ghidorah is a very popular kaiju, it has not been featured in its own film like Godzilla, Mothra, or Rodan.

Filmography

1. *Ghidorah, the Three-Headed Monster* (1964)
2. *Invasion of Astro-Monster* (1965)
3. *Destroy All Monsters* (1968)
4. *Godzilla vs. Gigan* (1972)
5. *Godzilla vs. King Ghidorah* (1991)
6. *Rebirth of Mothra III* (1998)
7. *Godzilla, Mothra and King Ghidorah: Giant Monsters All-Out Attack* (2001)

Original movie poster for *Ghidorah, the Three-Headed Monster* (1964)

Production Company: Toho | **STATS Height:** Up to 100m / **Weight:** Up to 60,000 tons / **Flight speed:** N/A / **Origin:** Indeterminate | **Powers:** Atomic ray / Nuclear pulse / Super regeneration / Magnetic electricity force

天然色 **三大怪獣**
地球最大の決戦

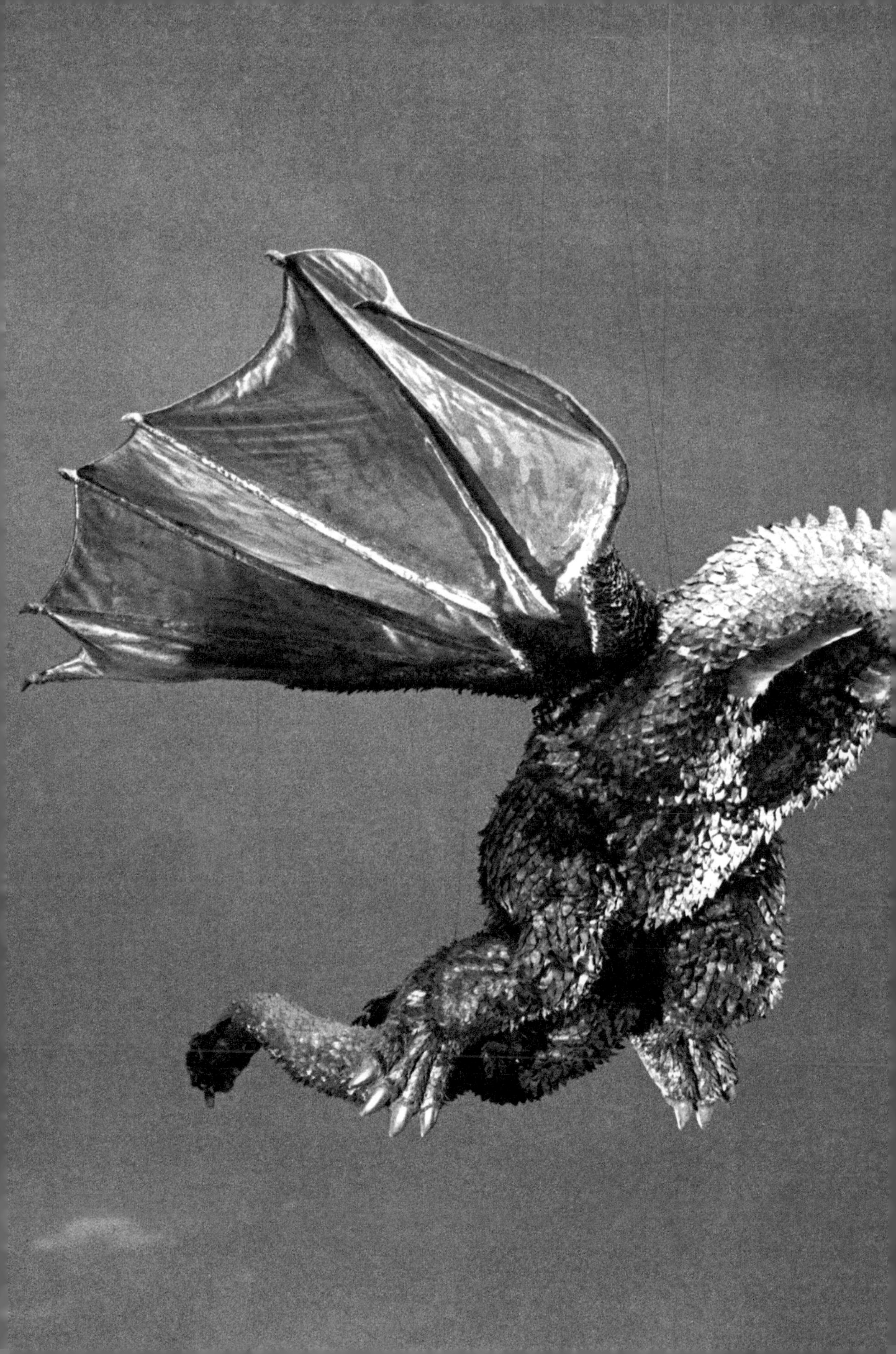

Unlike other kaiju that were played by suited actors, King Ghidorah required individual maneuvering of the three dragon heads. In most scenes the kaiju is flying, which added another magnitude of complexity to animating the character. Executing such a demanding production represents the height of special effects expertise at that time. Shown here is a view of the set in *Ghidorah, the Three-Headed Monster* (1964). **Following spread:** King Ghidorah in *Destroy All Monsters* (1968).

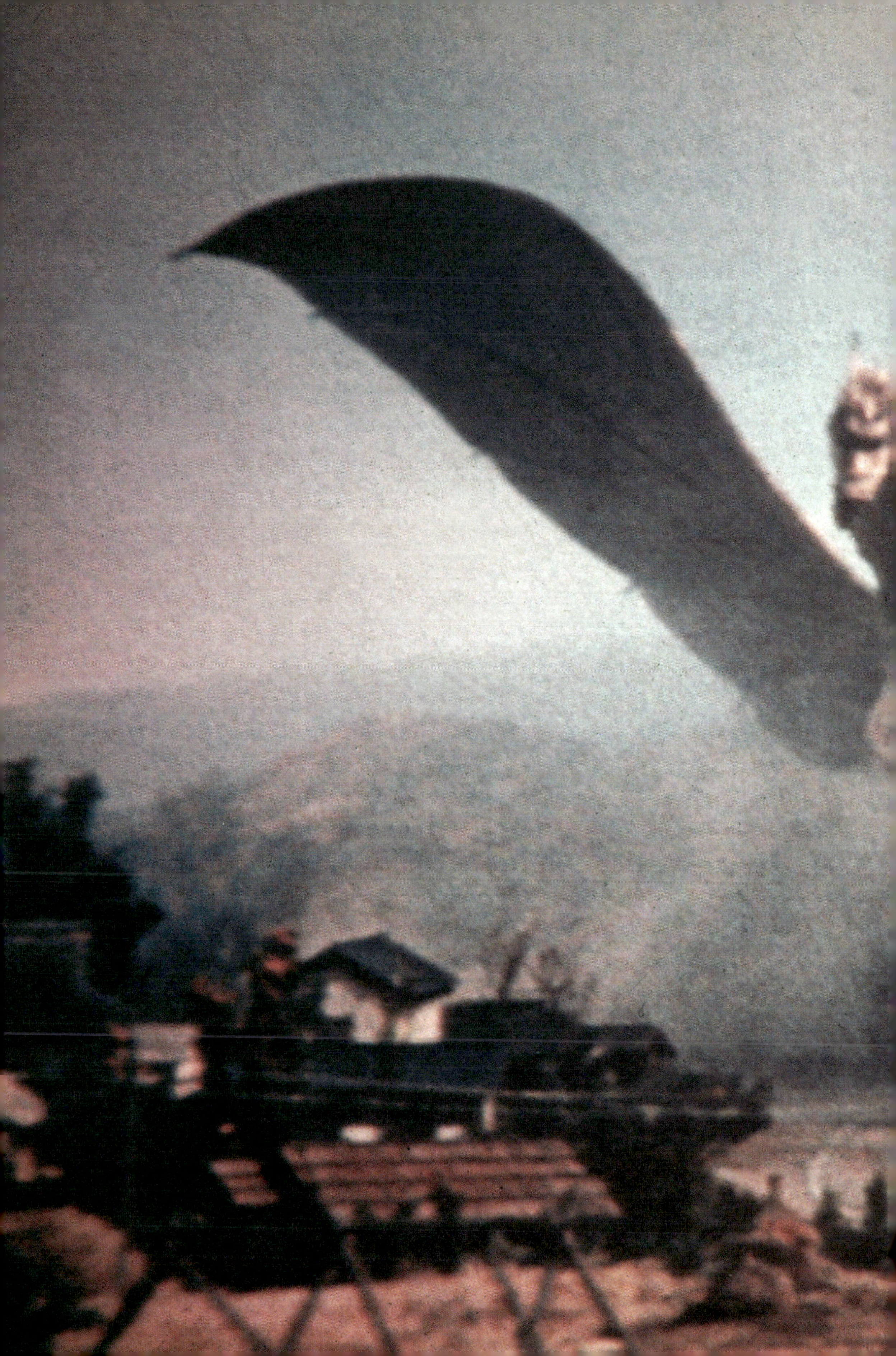

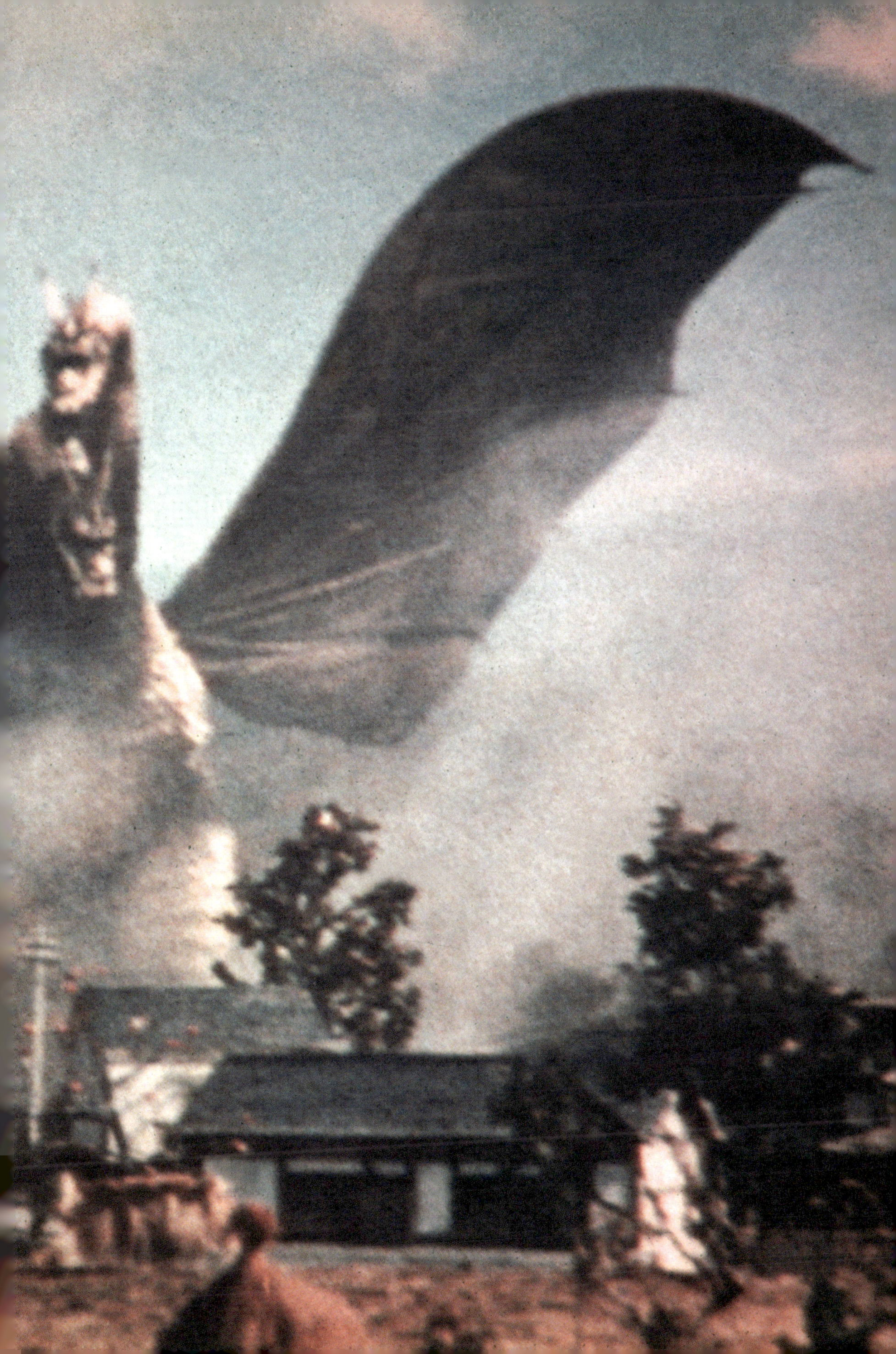

ラドン
Rodan

Rodan made its first appearance in an eponymously titled film. Along with Godzilla and Mothra, Rodan is one of the three big Toho kaiju. Rodan's name is a simplified version of "pteranodon," which was a large, tailless, winged pterosaur of the Cretaceous period. Rodan is a winged dragon (with the addition of gnashing teeth) that lived in the Mesozoic Period. It is reanimated deep in the recesses of a coal shaft in Japan's south island, where it hatched from an egg and took nutrients from ancient dragonfly larvae. Radiation from nuclear testing and high temperatures from volcanic gases helped incubate the egg. In the first film, it remains unclear whether there are multiples of Rodan. We don't see a scene where there are more than one kaiju on the screen at a time, though the story line hints at multiples. There are some discrepancies in the basic backstory of the two films—within Rodan's filmography in general there are a number of conflicting story lines. (In the foreign release of the film a scene was added to clearly show there are two kaiju Rodans.) At the end of the film, Rodan uses its homing instinct to return to Aso Mountain, where it is attacked with missiles by the military. Aso mountain erupts as a result and envelops Rodan in magma. As with several other Toho characters, the figure's head was created by Teizoh Toshimitu and the torso by the Yagi brothers.

Rodan is certainly a strong opponent. It has the ability to fly at such great speeds that it creates a sonic boom capable of toppling buildings. Rodan makes its second film appearance in *Ghidorah, the Three-Headed Monster*, and is pitted against Godzilla. In *Godzilla vs. Mechagodzilla*, Godzilla's heat beam turns Rodan into Fire Rodan (a creature capable of spitting a uranium heat ray). The monster, nonetheless, lacks the intriguing nature or ominous portent of a character such as Hedorah. Rodan's presence has more to do with brute force and barbarism of spirit. Rodan's voice is a sound effect that mixes contrabass with a human voice, giving the character a sirenlike quality.

Filmography
1. *Rodan* (1956)
2. *Ghidorah, the Three-Headed Monster* (1964)
3. *Invasion of Astro-Monster* (1965)
4. *Destroy All Monsters* (1968)
5. *Godzilla vs. Mechagodzilla* (1993)
6. *Godzilla Final Wars* (2004)

Rodan enjoys a meal in the 1956 eponymous release.

Production Company: Toho | **STATS Height:** Up to 100m / **Weight:** Up to 30,000 tons / **Flight speed:** Mach 15 / **Origin:** Coal mine in Kitamatsu | **Powers:** Hurricane winds / Spikes on chest

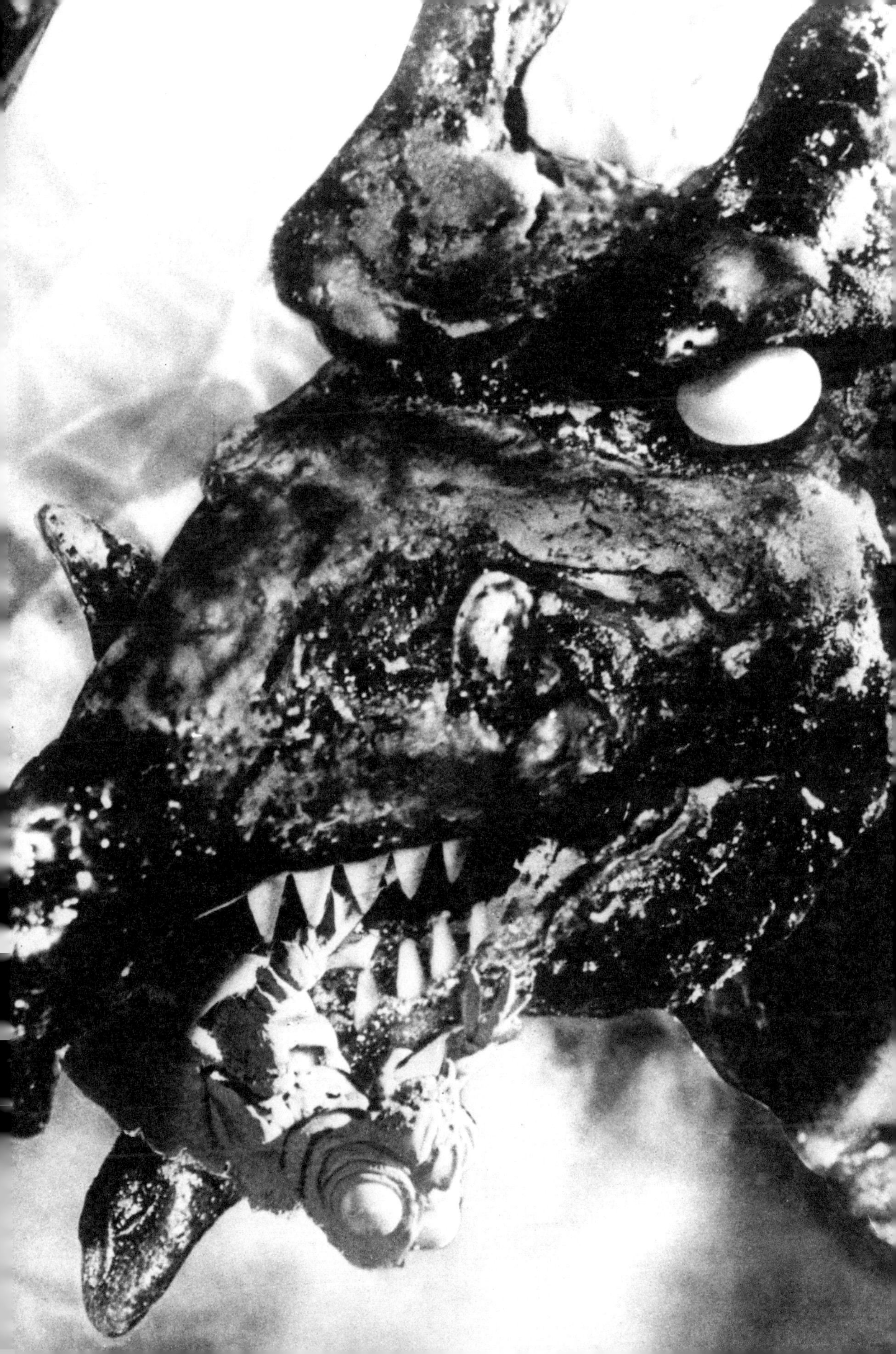

Godzilla, King of Monsters, does not make an appearance in *Rodan* (1956). The film is instead devoted to the story of a winged dragon that is brought back to life by radiation from nuclear testing and high geological temperatures.

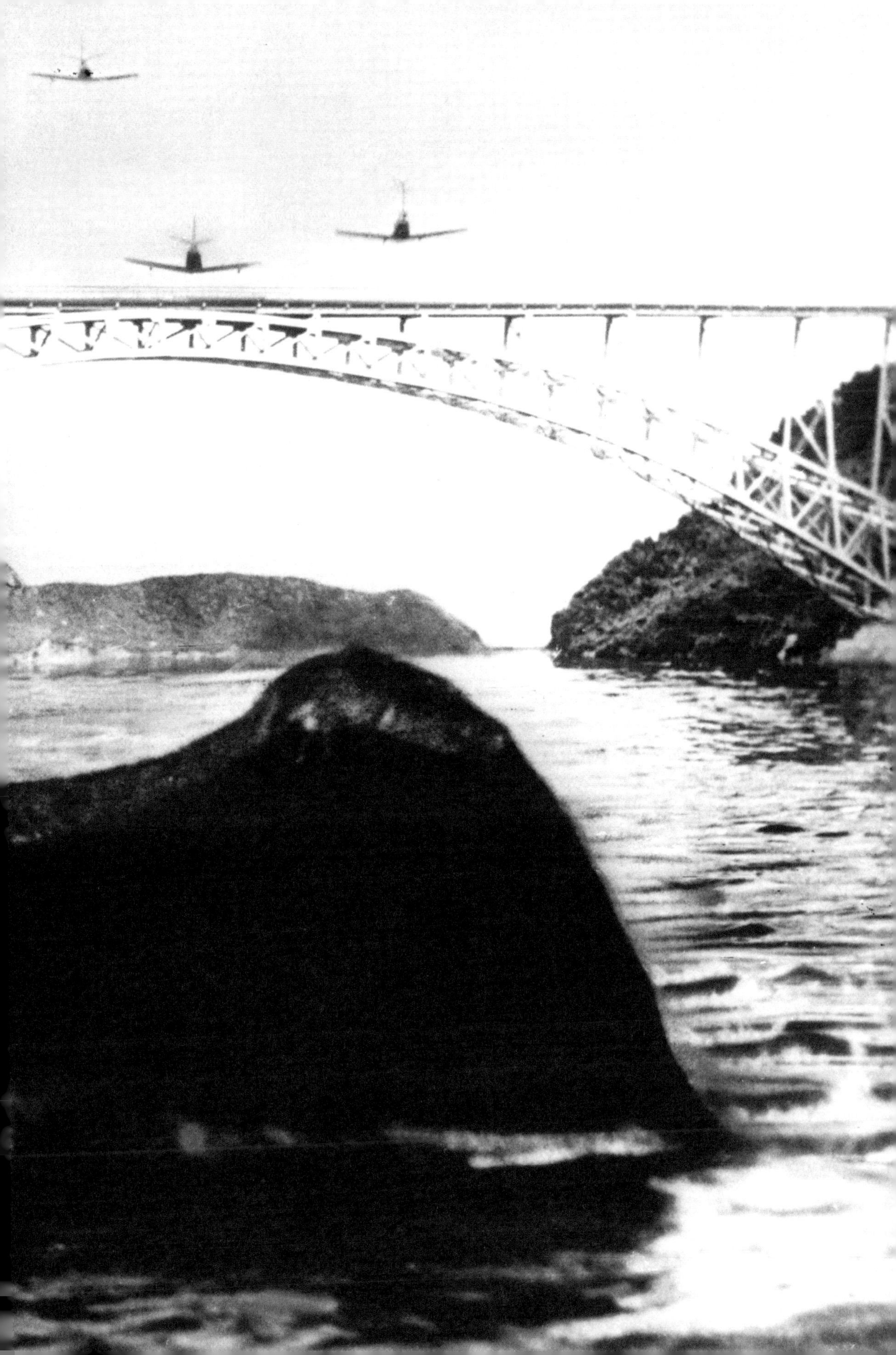

Megalon

Megalon is a beetle-shaped kaiju that appeared in *Godzilla vs. Megalon* and the television series *Godzilla Island*. Its forearms form the two halves of a drill, which it places together to bore into the ground's surface. It also has wings for flight. From its mouth it can throw napalm bombs; from the tip of its horn it can fire a deadly laser beam. Before Megalon is introduced, the film focuses on the underwater kingdom of Seatopia. A subterranean nuclear test in the 1960s on Asuka Island of the Aleutian Chain damaged Seatopia. As a retaliatory measure, the Seatopians induced an earthquake and sent their guardian deity Megalon to the earth's surface to begin a rampage against the above-earth dwellers. The Seatopians are believed to be descend-ants of the people of Lemuria, a civilization thought to have been contemporaneous with Atlantis. The film informs us that their continent sank into the ocean some three million years ago and they have lived there ever since. Before calling upon Megalon the Seatopians steal a robot, Jet Jaguar, from the humans. The robot is eventually recovered and when things begin to look bleak for the Seatopians they summon another kaiju, Gigan, to do battle. Soon after, Godzilla also appears and engages in a tag match battle, which ends with Megalon escaping to Seatopia.

This film was shot in only two weeks on a limited budget. As a result there was a limitation in the number of principal actors. This is the only film in the Godzilla series that doesn't feature a woman in the main cast. (In these early films the female lead is either a reporter, radio operator, or photographer who witnesses events while also becoming involved in the story's development midway through.) It was part of the Toho Champion Festival of films (1969–1978). When this film was released, hero-driven television programs (such as *Masked Raider*) were quite popular. Their influence can be seen in *Megalon*, with the orches-tration of the theme music or in the design of Jet Jaguar. The only scene where Megalon does exhibit some dynamic force is in the destruction of a dam. This was an isolated spectacle in an otherwise underwhelming action production.

Filmography

1. *Godzilla vs. Megalon* (1973)
2. *Godzilla Island* (television series, 1997–1998)

Megalon about to engage in battle in *Godzilla vs. Megalon* (1973).

Production Company: Toho | **STATS Height:** 55m / **Weight:** 40,000 tons / **Flight speed:** Mach 3 / **Origin:** Extraterrestrial | **Powers:** Red napalm bombs / Electrical beams / Magnetic vortex / Drill arms

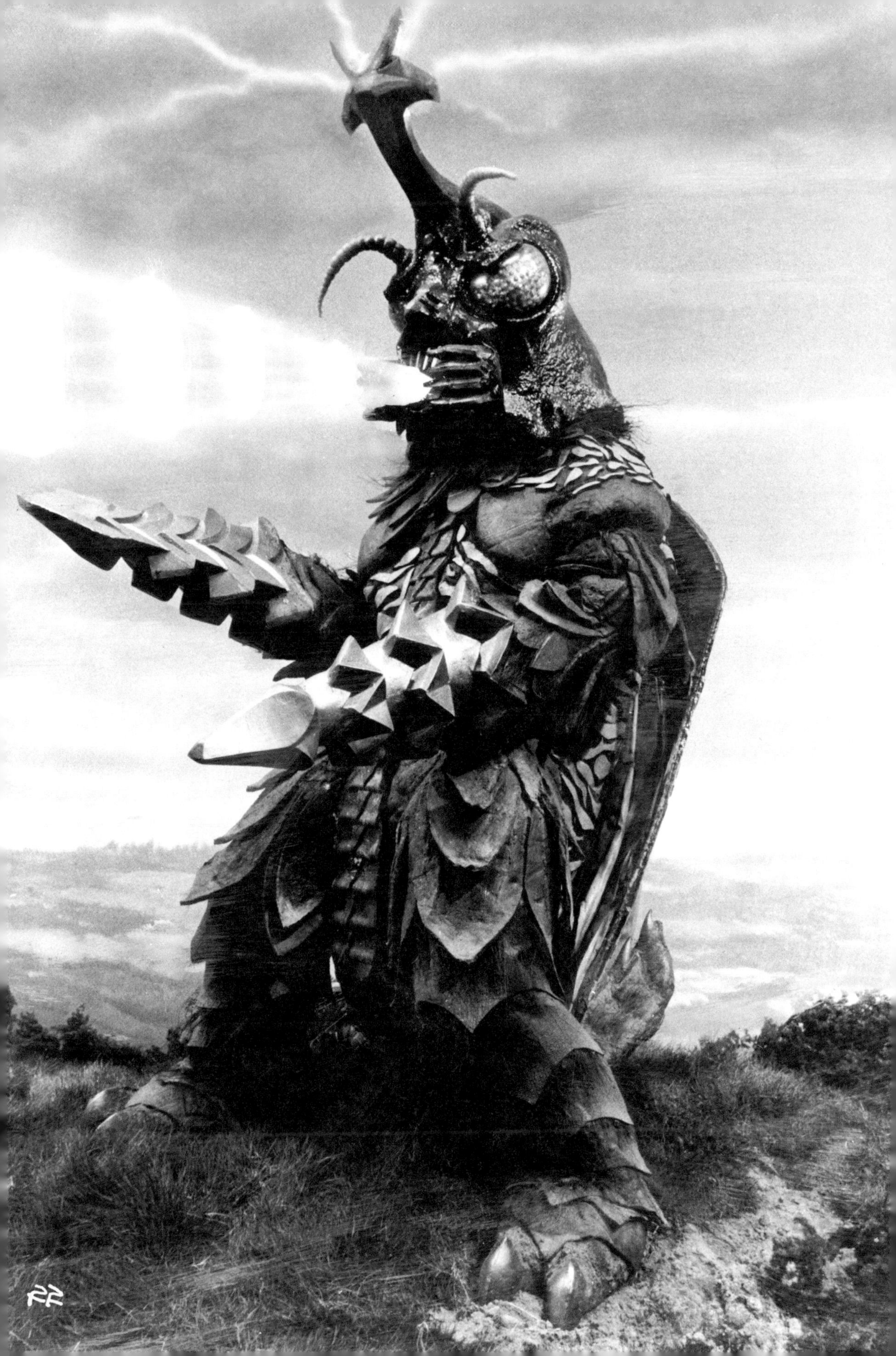

Megalon and Gigan team up to defeat the robot Jet Jaguar in a scene from *Godzilla vs. Megalon* (1973).

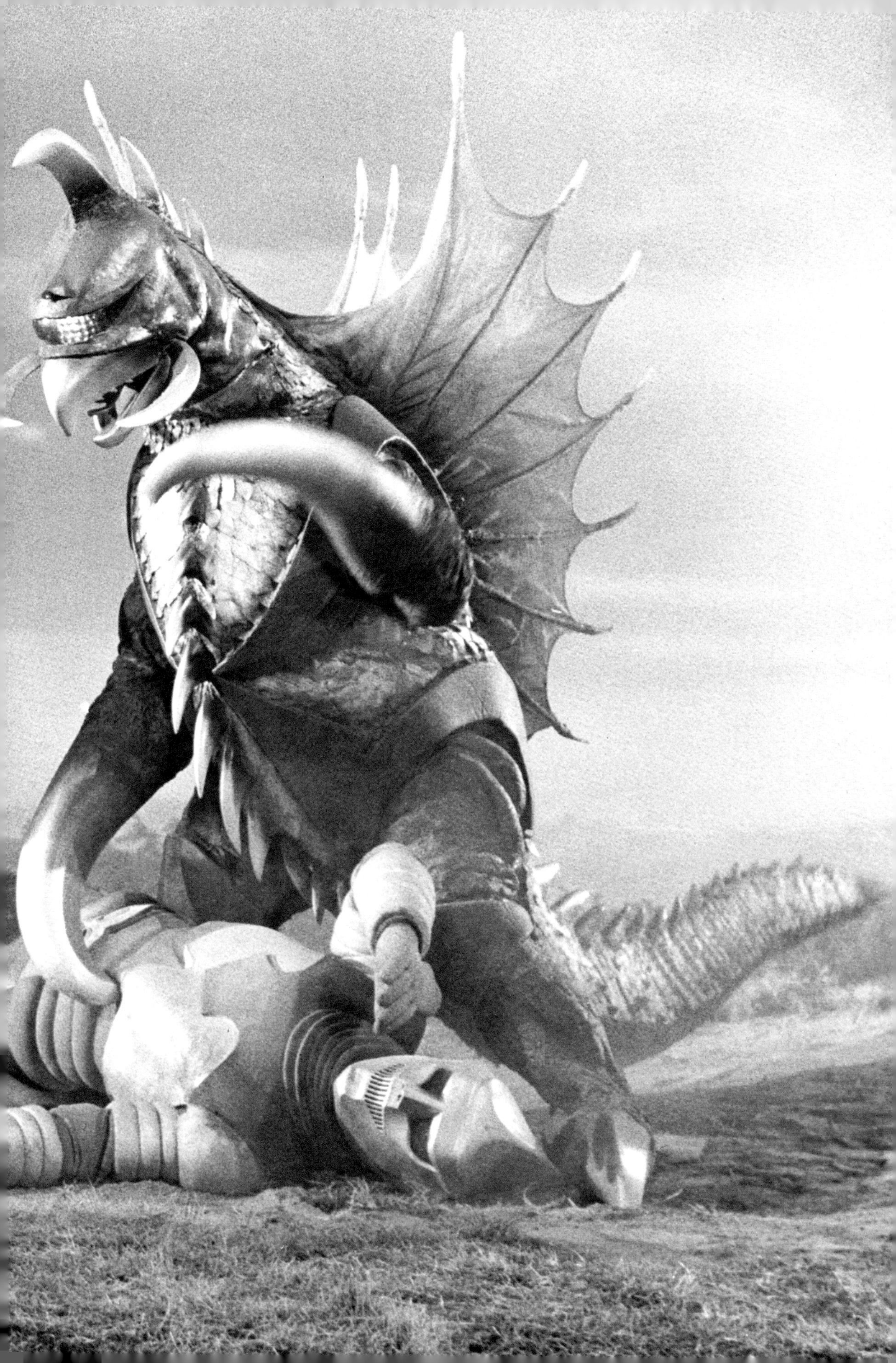

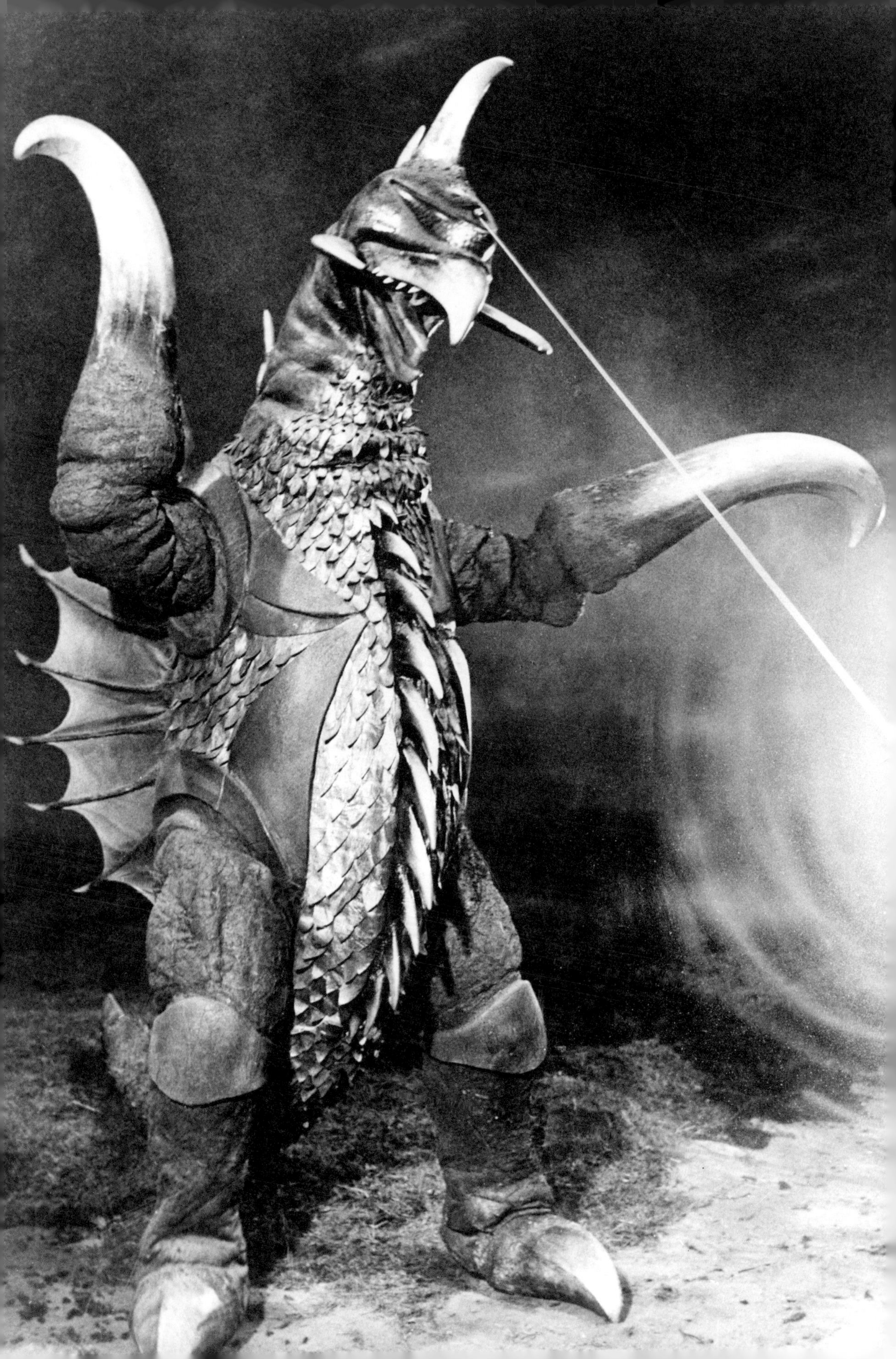

ガイガン

Gigan

Gigan is a cyborg kaiju that appeared in only three movies. The first was the 1972 *Godzilla vs. Gigan*. As a cyborg kaiju, Gigan is distinct from all the other kaiju in the Godzilla series. It has a single eye and a large horn. Sicklelike hooks that serve as forearms extend from its elbows. It has a spinning saw in its midsection and a light ray cannon embed-ded in its forehead. Gigan is capable of antigravity flight and teleportation (accompanied with a green pulse of light). On its back it has three fins and some type of protective structures on its appendages. It often pairs up with other kaiju in joint battle. Combining such an awesome appearance with ferocious fighting ability, it has endeared itself to many fans. Gigan had a range of abilities and features that made it a formidable enough opponent when it first appeared on the screen. In *Godzilla Final Wars* (2004), it is fitted with jetpacks for flight, grappling cables, razor-cutting disks, and an eye beam that is something like a power laser. Gigan is a cyborg, so these additional mechanics further emphasize the unusual qualities of this kaiju that make it unique in the genre. Despite its limited appearances in the series and the comparatively poor showing of the first two films, Gigan remains a popular character among fans. Gigan wasn't given the opportunity to change sides and act as a force for good (as is somewhat commonplace with other major kaiju characters, including Godzilla). This is a point made clear in the first of Gigan's two Showa-era films (*Godzilla vs. Gigan*), where Godzilla teams up with erstwhile rival Anguirus to thwart Gigan's attempt to destroy Tokyo. Gigan is first called into service by the alien race Nebula M Space Hunters because pollution on their own planet has made it uninhabitable. The following year, Gigan returned to polish off mankind in *Godzilla vs. Megalon*, but this was another attack that was thwarted by Godzilla. Gigan's distinctive silhouette (an amalgam of parts of different animals) and its cyborg nature make this character a memorable departure from the standards of kaiju character design.

Filmography
1. *Godzilla vs. Gigan* (1972)
2. *Godzilla vs. Megalon* (1973)
3. *Godzilla Final Wars* (2004)

Gigan attacks in *Godzilla vs. Gigan* (1972).

Production Company: Toho | **STATS Height:** Up to 120m / **Weight:** Up to 60,000 tons / **Flight speed:** Mach 3 / **Origin:** Prehistoric turtle created by Atlantians
Powers: Abdominal buzz saw / Cluster Beam / Grappling Hooks / Chainsaw Hand

A scene from *Godzilla vs. Gigan* (1972) featuring Godzilla, Gigan, and King Ghidorah.

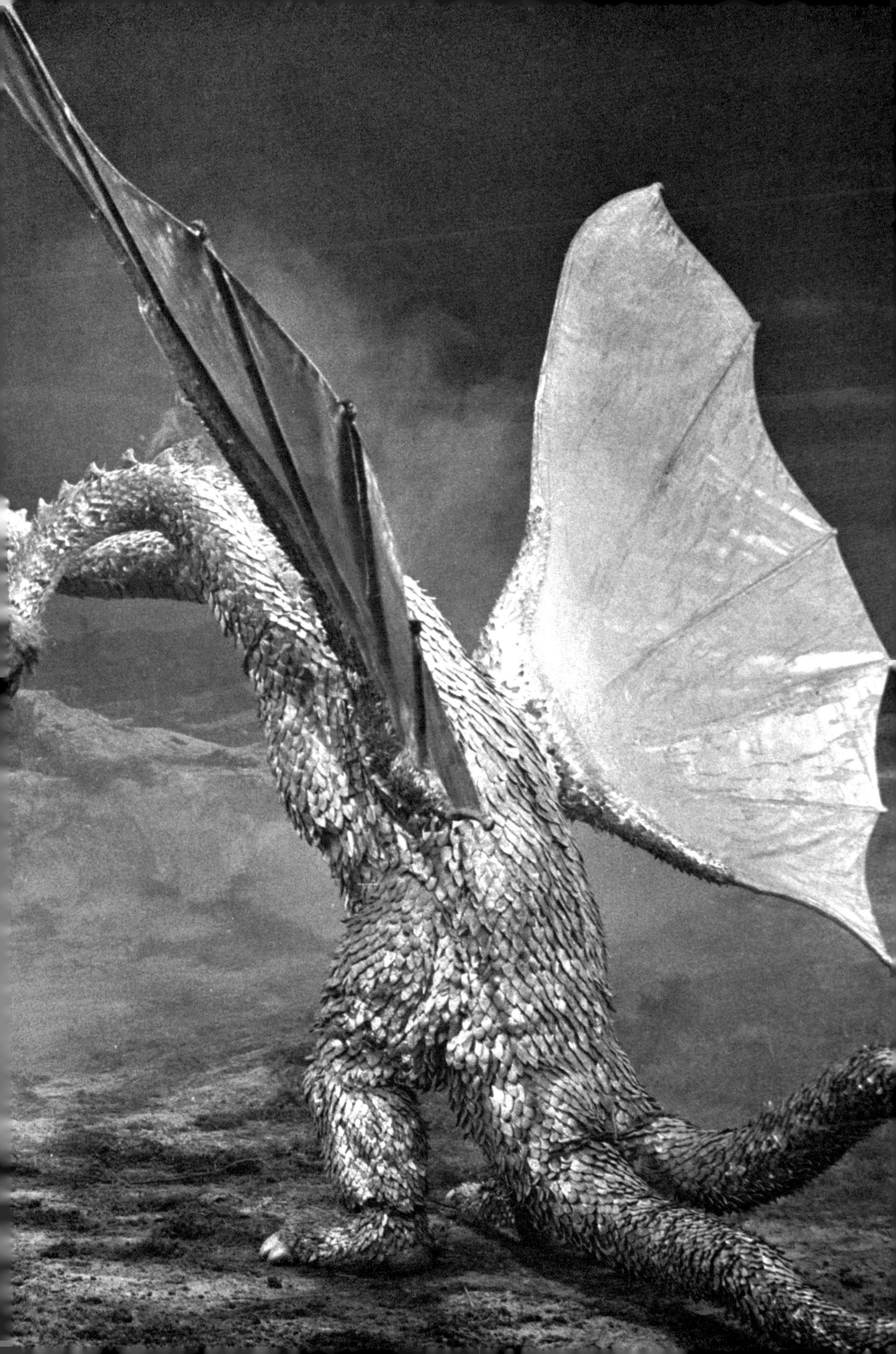

In *Godzilla Final Wars* (2004) a Gigan endowed with even more ferocious powers makes a fiery entrance.

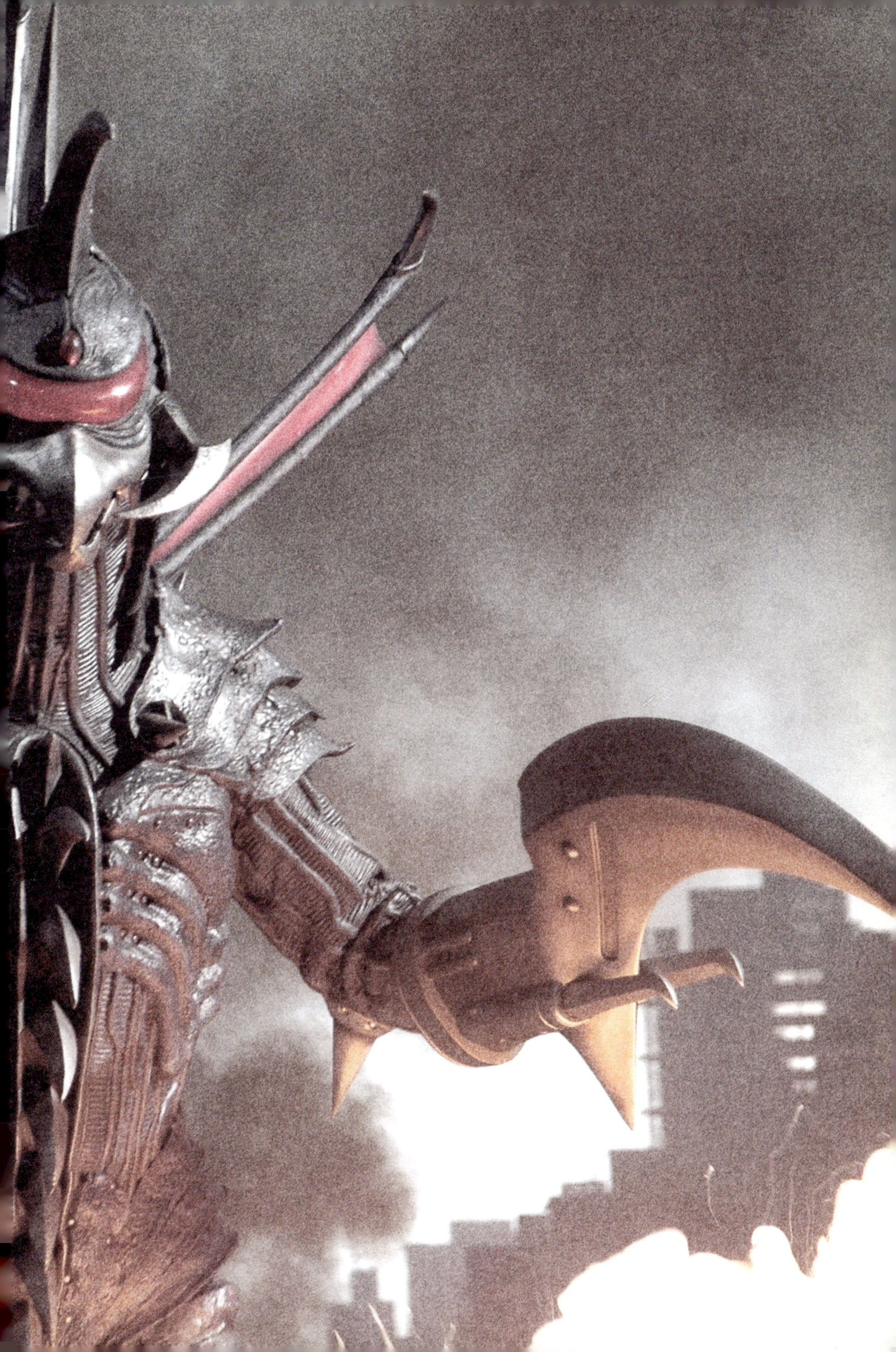

ミニラ
Minilla

Minilla is the child of Godzilla and first appeared in the film *Son of Godzilla* (1967). The name, which in Japanese is "Minira," is a conflation of "mini" and the "ra" of "Gojira" (which is how Godzilla is pronounced in Japanese). The Kewpie-shaped Minilla is colored mostly white with smooth and slippery skin. Minilla is much smaller than its ferocious parental figure Godzilla. Elements of Godzilla's characteristic brow are evident in the young kaiju's head construction while it's made more expressive (the creature seems to be perpetually smiling). Minilla is able to spit heat rays from its mouth. Unlike the continuous blasts that Godzilla can let out, its diminutive protégé shoots something resembling smoke rings. If you step on its tail the shock prompts emission of these heat rays. Minilla does not earn accolades as an exemplary warrior in the Godzilla series of films. Some young viewers identified with the character but many fans were disgruntled with the studio's attempt to overtly pander to young children at the expense of fight-driven screen action. Minilla does possess some abilities (such as blowing atomic smoke rings and communicating with Godzilla over vast distances via brainwaves).

Minilla was buried in Sogell Island while still in the egg. During its incubation it was exposed to special electrical waves. Kamacuras, another Toho kaiju, digs up the egg and breaks the shell (resulting in Minilla's birth). Godzilla—acting as a surrogate parent—raises the tyke and teaches him to shoot heat rays. Instead of developing strictly as a sidekick, Minilla remains a somewhat independent character. In the conclusion of the first film, Minilla and Godzilla are caught in a weather experiment that blankets the island with snow and freezes the two kaiju. This is a solemn and oddly somber wrap-up for a production meant to launch a character that would draw in younger viewers.

Filmography
1. *Son of Godzilla* (1967)
2. *Destroy All Monsters* (1968)
3. *All Monsters Attack* (1969)
4. *Godzilla Final Wars* (2004)

Goazilla with its adopted child Minilla in *Son of Godzilla* (1967).

Production Company: Toho | **STATS Height:** Up to 20m / **Weight:** Up to 30,000 tons / **Flight speed:** N/A / **Origin:** Hatched from an egg on Sogell Island | **Powers:** Radioactive smoke rings / Atomic ray / Radio brainwave communication / Can shrink to human size

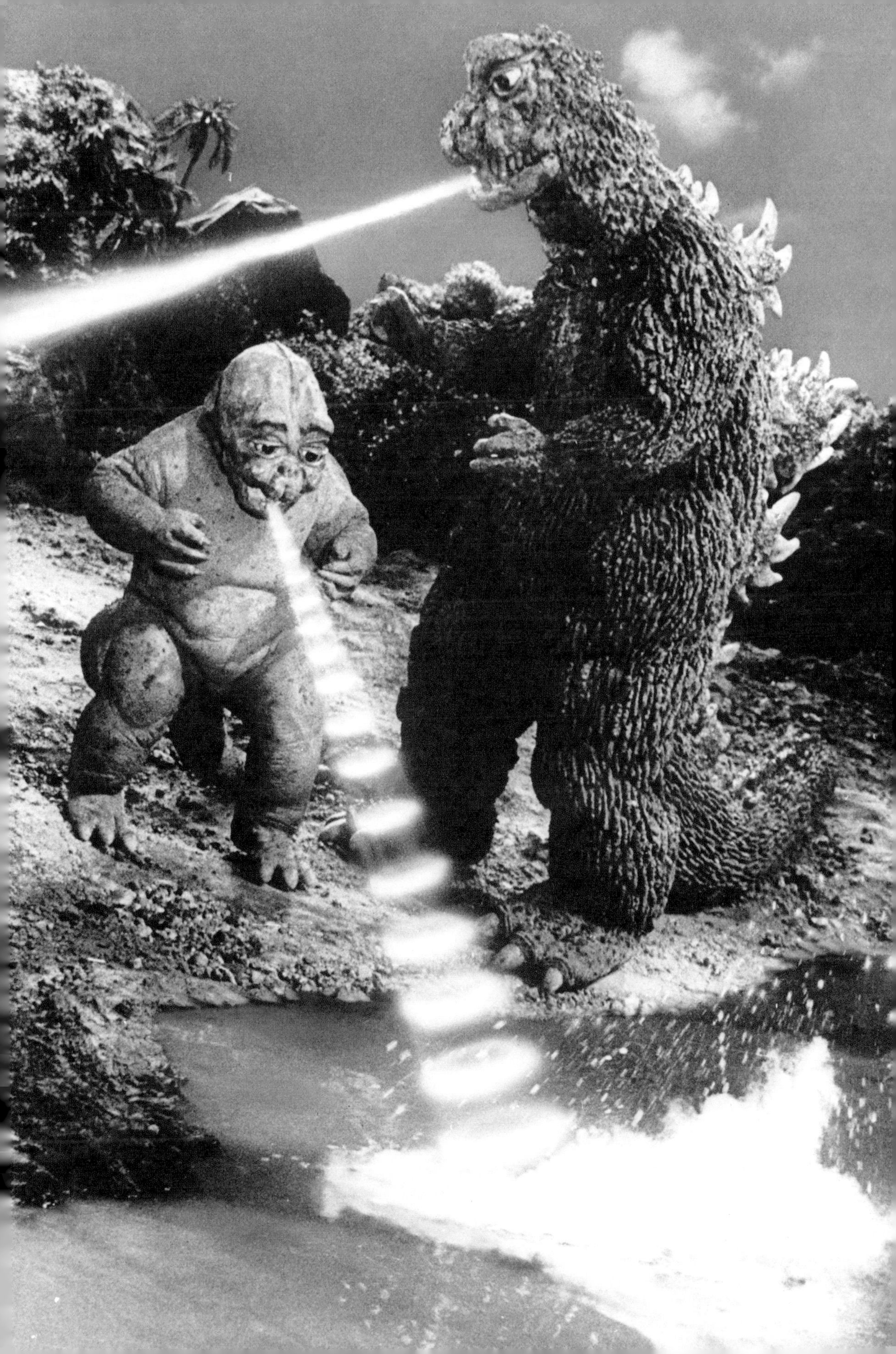

Minilla's supporting role in *Godzilla Final Wars* (2004) is true to form. While it does little to advance the main action, its inclusion in the final film in the Godzilla series acknowledges Minilla's relative importance in the cumulative history of the productions.

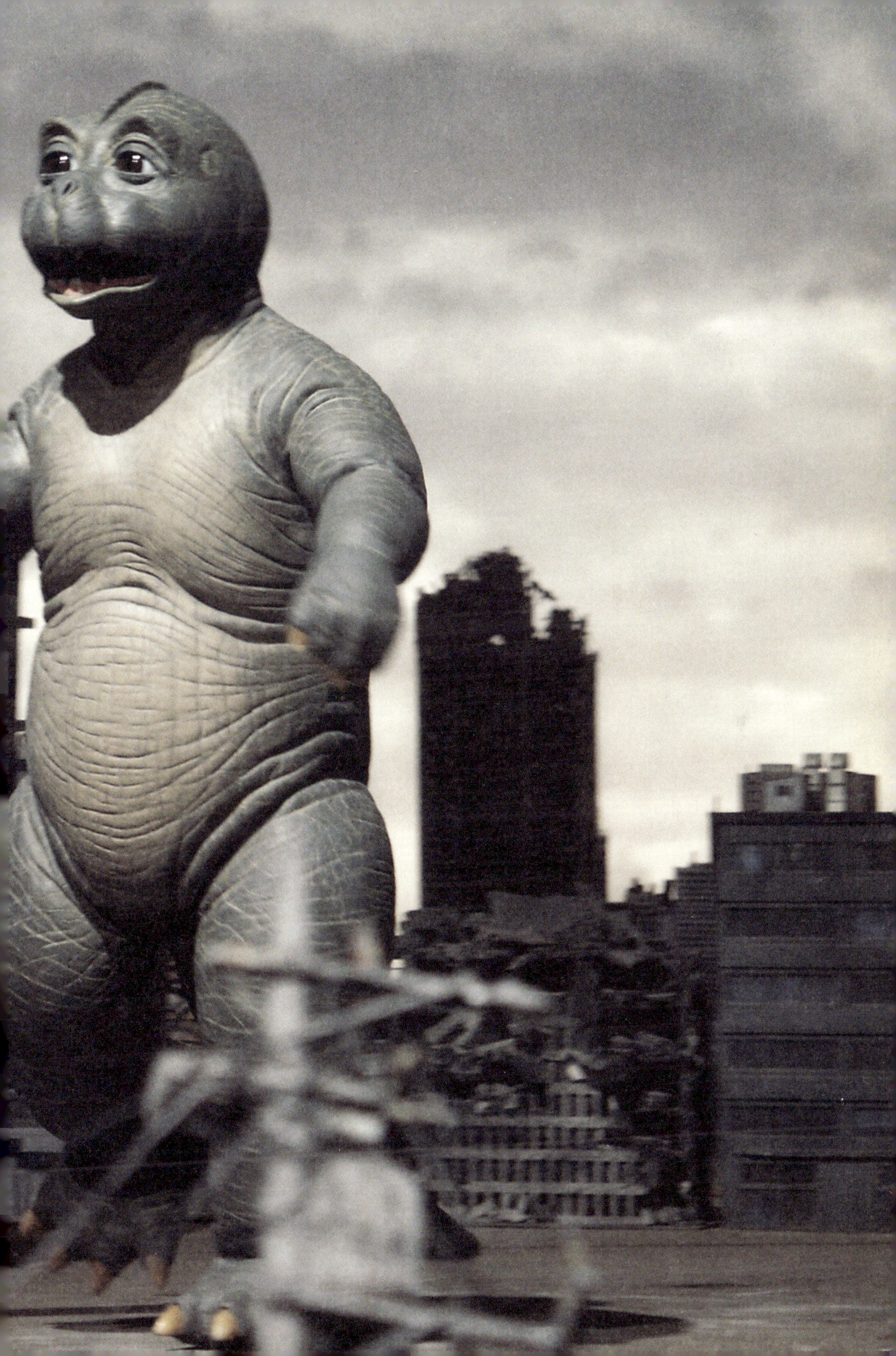

GAMERA VS BARUGON

ガメラ
Gamera

Gamera was first introduced in *Daikaiju Gamera*, a film released in 1965 by Daiei (today known as Kadokawa Eiga). The film kicked off a long series of film productions pitting the dai-kaiju (big kaiju) Gamera against other kaiju in battle. Seeing the phenomenal success Toho enjoyed with the first installments of their Godzilla films, nearly every film company was prompted to create their own kaiju productions. Of the crop of new recruits, Gamera was one of the few contenders in the market that jostled with Godzilla for the title of most popular kaiju in Japan. While the two studios battled for ticket sales revenue, their on-screen characters never sparred in battle. Together the two—*Gamera* and *Godzilla*—are the two longest-running and popular kaiju film series in Japan.

According to Eskimo folklore, Gamera is a kaiju that was slumbering in ice at the North Pole. Another story informs us that the creature used to live on the continent of Atlantis. As the result of the explosion of a nuclear warhead (fired by some unspecified country) the ice in which Gamera was frozen is shattered and the monster awakens. It heads south and eventually comes to Japan, where it goes on an extensive rampage. In the first production, Gamera's character is violent. In order to appeal to children, in subsequent films Gamera rescues children whenever they are in peril. Daiei successfully exploited this formula—Gamera battling evil kaiju as a hero to children—to solidify its stronghold with its core fan base of young children. There was always a young non-Japanese boy or non-Japanese family among the cast in the Daiei period. These characters would engage in adventures with the protagonist, who was always a young Japanese boy.

Gamera's design was a humorous take on the turtle (with added features such as the ability to fly). The gigantic turtle's back featured layered scales. Two tusks thrust outward and upward from both sides of its lower chin. Gamera has green blood. As with an actual turtle, its head, appendages, and tail can be pulled into its shell for protection. When in such a form, Gamera is capable of shooting fireballs and generating enough thrust power to propel itself through the atmosphere (as well as outer space) at a top speed of Mach 3. Gamera can not only rotate in mid-flight but also fly in any direction without the need to turn, allowing it to shoot fireballs from four directions. In later films it was revealed that Gamera was capable of shooting plasma fireballs and extensions of the bones in its elbows serve as "elbow claws." Inside Gamera there is something akin to a power plant that produces the heat required for its blasts of fire. The creature subsists on a diet of magma, high-voltage electricity, coal, petroleum, and uranium (reserves of which it stores inside its body in special compartments) in order to provide fuel for its armory.

Gamera vs. Barugon (1966).

Production Company: Toho | **STATS Height:** Up to 80m / **Weight:** Up to 120,000 tons / **Flight speed:** Mach 3 / **Origin:** Extraterrestrial / **Powers:** Fire breath / Impenetrable shell / Regenerative coma

Despite being basically a turtle, Gamera is capable of flying up to speeds of Mach 3. After a debut as a fearsome monster, its character was developed as a friend and even hero to young boys.

ガメラ対宇宙怪獣バイラス

DAIEI COLOUR
GAMERA VS BARUGON

The second film in the Gamera series, *Gamera vs. Barugon*, was released in 1966. In this scene the kaiju are laying waste to parts of Osaka.

解剖図

KAIJU CROSS SECTIONS

by Shoji Ohtomo

Shoji Ohtomo (1936–1973) worked as an editor, sci-fi writer, movie critic, and translator. He is best known, however, as "Dr. Kaiju" for his numerous drawings of kaiju figure cross sections. Throughout the 1960s and 1970s he was intensely involved in helping to develop characters and weapons for kaiju television series, most notably Eiji Tsuburaya's productions such as *Ultra Q* and the *Ultraman* series. His illustrated encyclopedia of kaiju called *Kaiju Zukan* (Akida Shoten) was published in 1966 and became a cult classic. The book was comprised of the kaiju features from *Shonen Sunday* and *Shonen Magajin* and is said to have been the first book purchased by the current crown prince of Japan as a child. Ohtomo was one of the first *otaku* (someone with obsessive interests, particularly in fantasy stories such as manga and anime). In addition to his work with kaiju, he was involved with writing for the children's show *Topo Gigio*. Through his work as a writer and editor in the children's genre for publishers Kodansha, Shokanka, Asahi Sonorama, and Akita Shoten, Ohtomo made an indelible mark on a whole generation of young Japanese in the Showa era (1926–1989). His areas of expertise extended to literature, history, science, music, art, and agriculture—all themes that he introduced into the young adult magazines on which he worked as an art director. His cross-section approach to displaying information also included elaborate scenes of ships in the water, cross sections of homes and machinery, and sundry illustrations of pop culture. In an era of rapid economic development in Japan there was a keen interest in all things related to the future, science, and technology. Ohtomo's ability to render complexity of detail with a high level of accessibility gave his illustrations an across-the-board appeal. He signed his illustrations "OH" in a logotype fashion.

In 1963 (at the age of twenty-six), he started a series of interviews for *SF* magazine about the creators of sci-fi. In the same year he served as director of the newly established Science Fiction and Fantasy Writers of Japan. In 1970, he served as director of the International SF Symposium in Japan. Ohtomo became involved with Tsuburaya Productions when *Ultra Q* was still in the proposal phase and helped create kaiju and alien characters.

He died suddenly at the age of 36 in 1973. After his death it was revealed that Otomo Shoji was a pseudonym and his real name was Toshiji Shishimoto. In 1988 the Ohtomo Shoji Award for Scenario Writers was established.

Translations for pages 81–88 are on page 89.

地底怪獣　テレスドン

- 目は光によわい →
- するどい鼻先で岩をほる
- するどい毒づめ
- 皮ふの強さは鋼鉄の二千倍
- マグマぶくろ（はきだすと火になる）
- 体内五カ所（頭、背、両腕、尾）にわかれた脳で、頭がきずついても平気でとびまわる。
- 尾の強さはブルドーザー10万台分
- ひふの厚さは60センチ
- 足の力は30階のビルをけり倒す

©円谷プロ

火炎怪獣　ガメラ

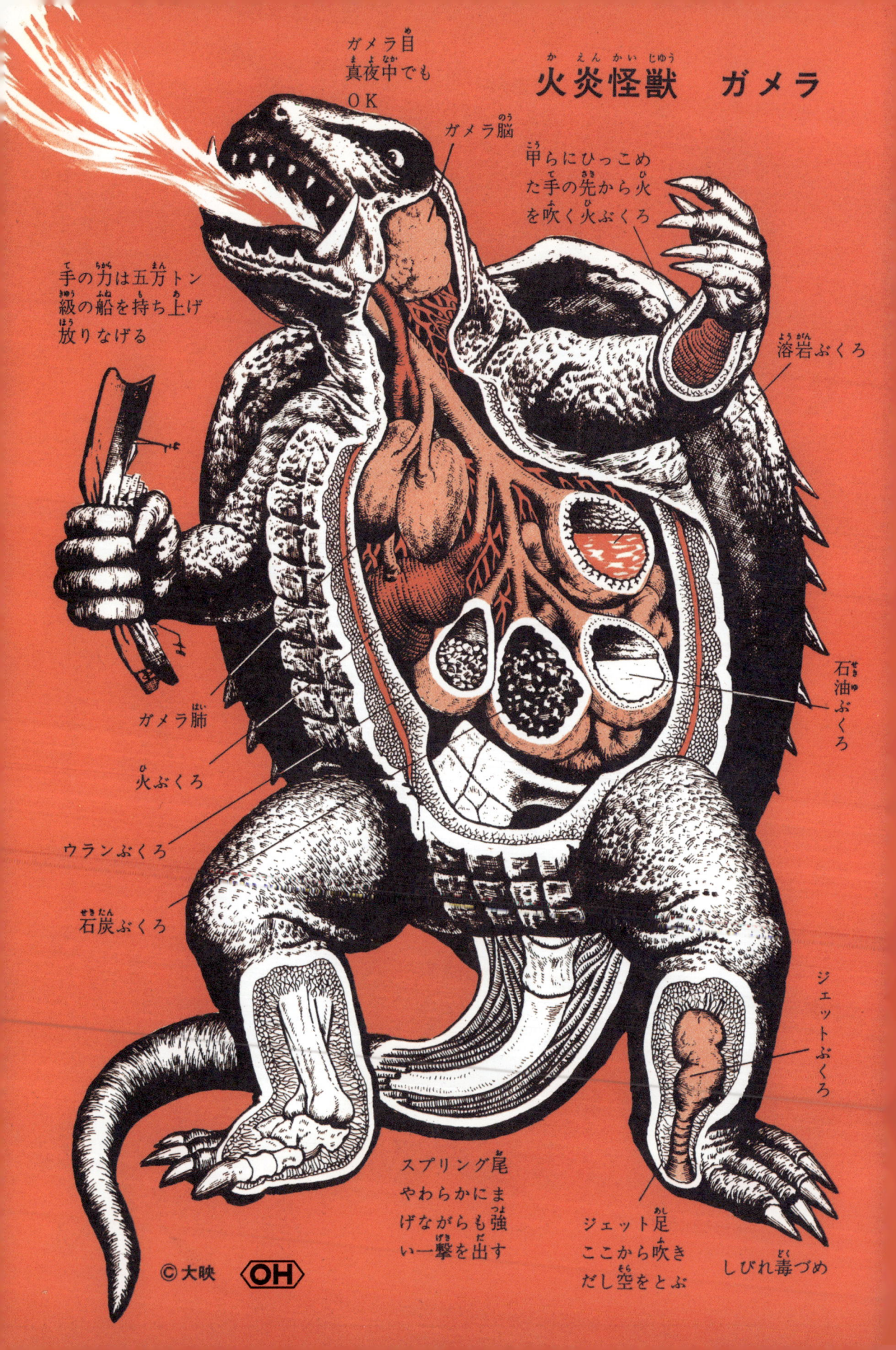

- ガメラ目　真夜中でもOK
- ガメラ脳
- 甲らにひっこめた手の先から火を吹く火ぶくろ
- 溶岩ぶくろ
- 手の力は五万トン級の船を持ち上げ放りなげる
- 石油ぶくろ
- ガメラ肺
- 火ぶくろ
- ウランぶくろ
- 石炭ぶくろ
- ジェットぶくろ
- スプリング尾　やわらかにまげながらも強い一撃を出す
- ジェット尻　ここから吹きだし空をとぶ
- しびれ毒づめ

©大映　OH

大巨獣 ガッパ

目と口から四千度の殺人爆発光線をだす

レーダー角、空をとぶかじとなる

宇宙線を集める角

どんな音でも聞きわけられるするどい耳

光線エネルギーぶくろ

ガッパ肺

毒ぶくろ

うろこは針やかみそりのようにするどい

タコ胃

鉄もひきさく爪

たべたタコ

ビルをメチャメチャにできる強力な尾

© 日活

殺人音波怪獣

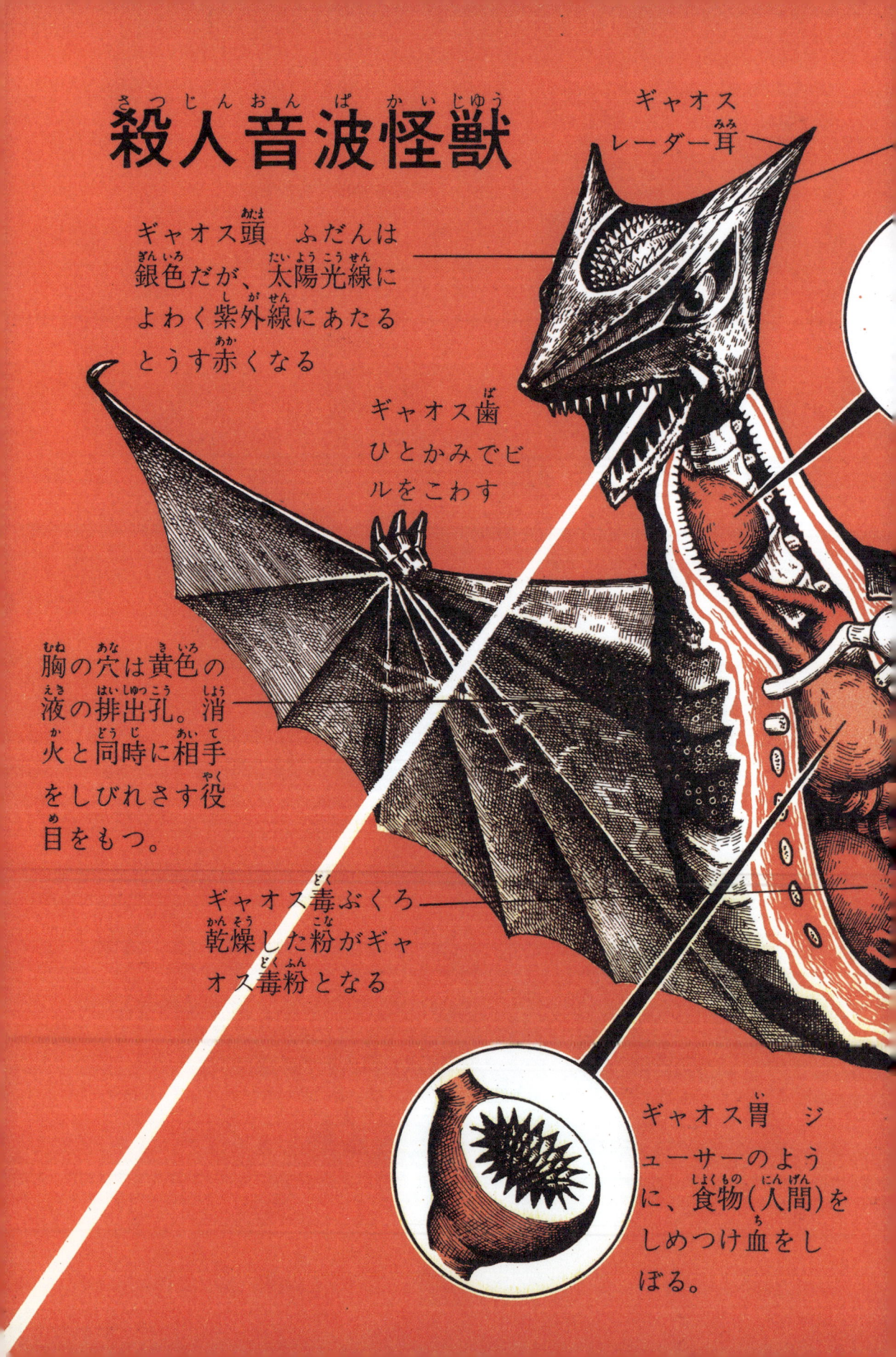

ギャオスレーダー耳

ギャオス頭 ふだんは銀色だが、太陽光線によわく紫外線にあたるとうす赤くなる

ギャオス歯 ひとかみでビルをこわす

胸の穴は黄色の液の排出孔。消火と同時に相手をしびれさす役目をもつ。

ギャオス毒ぶくろ 乾燥した粉がギャオス毒粉となる

ギャオス胃 ジューサーのように、食物(人間)をしめつけ血をしぼる。

ギャオス

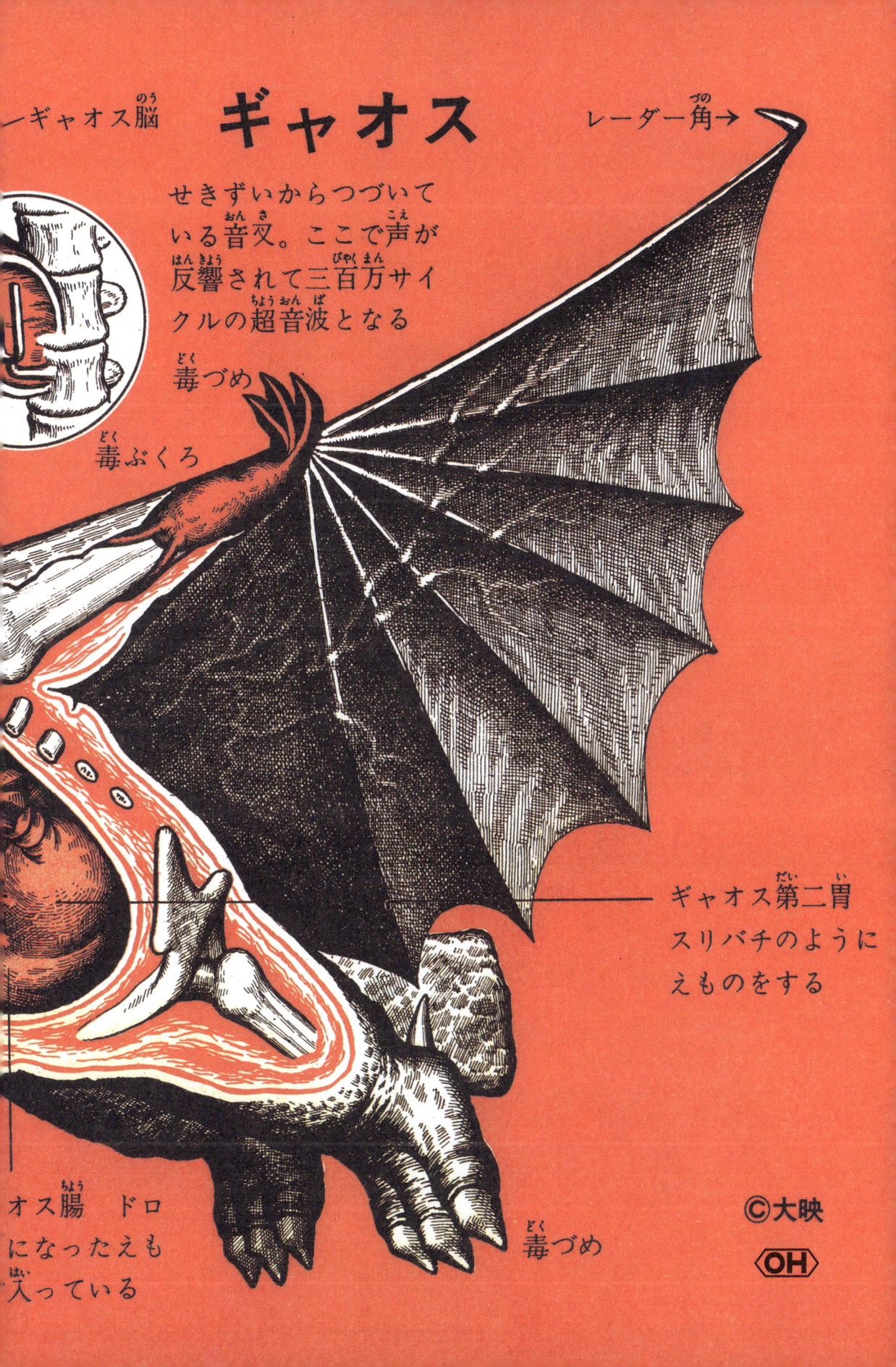

←ギャオス脳　　　　　　　　　　　　　　レーダー角→

せきずいからつづいて
いる音叉。ここで声が
反響されて三百万サイ
クルの超音波となる

毒づめ

毒ぶくろ

ギャオス第二胃
スリバチのように
えものをする

オス腸　ドロ
になったえも
入っている

毒づめ

Ⓒ大映

四次元怪獣　ブルトン

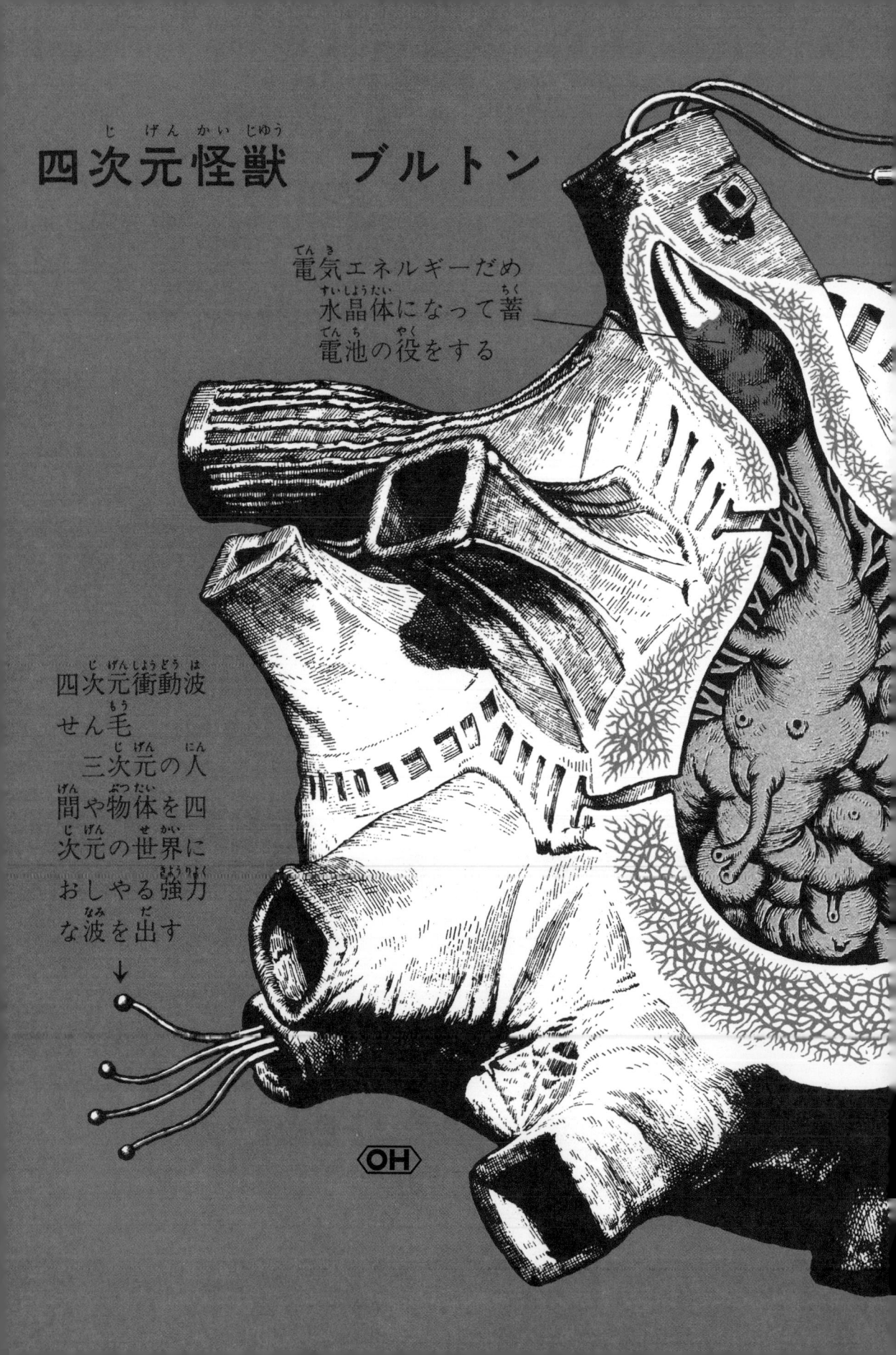

電気エネルギーだめ
水晶体になって蓄
電池の役をする

四次元衝動波
せん毛
三次元の人間や物体を四次元の世界におしやる強力な波を出す

←空中放電せん毛
レーザー光線を出して敵をもやす

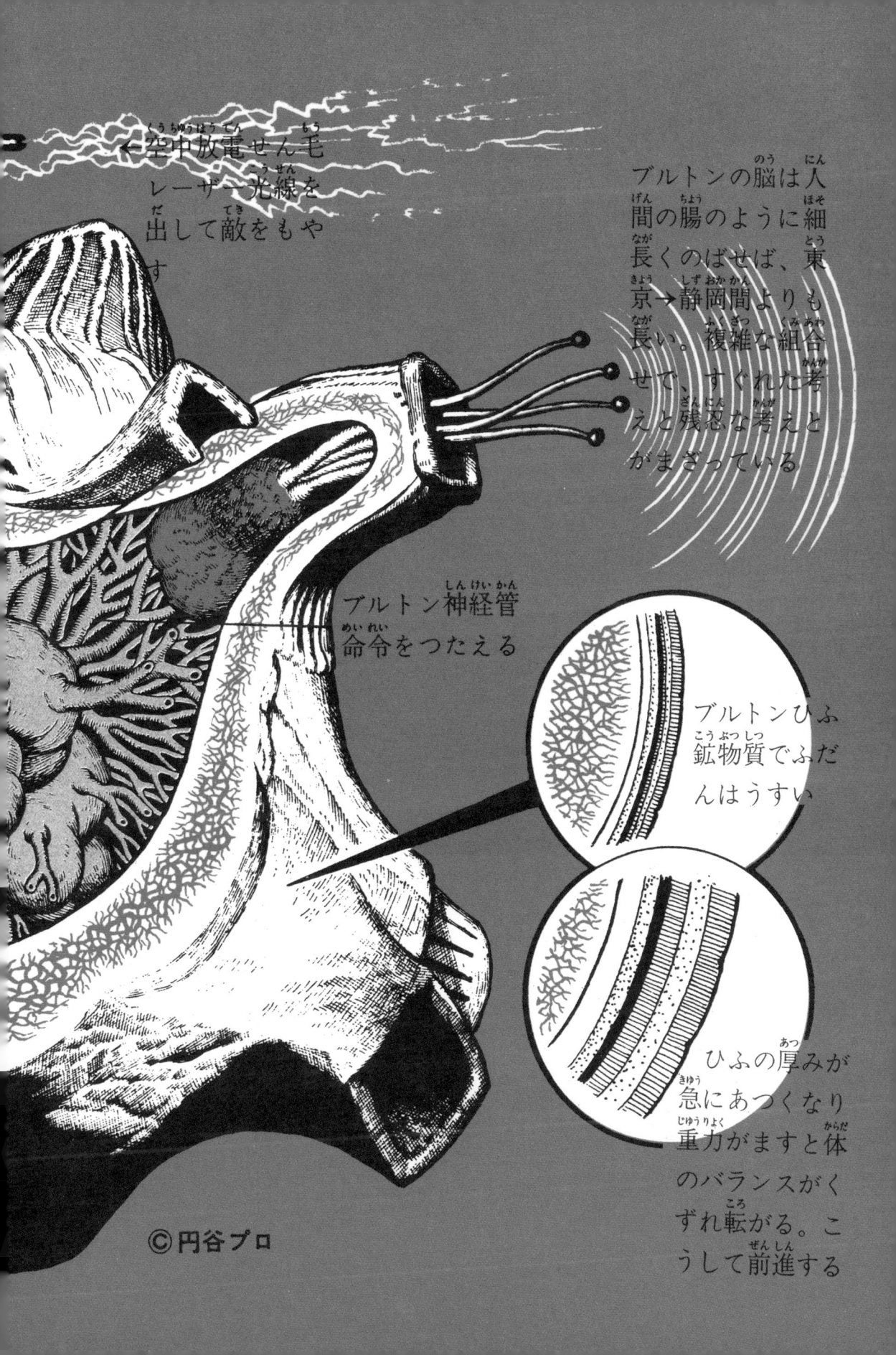

ブルトンの脳は人間の腸のように細長くのばせば、東京→静岡間よりも長い。複雑な組合せで、すぐれた考えと残忍な考えとがまざっている

ブルトン神経管
命令をつたえる

ブルトンひふ
鉱物質でふだんはうすい

ひふの厚みが急にあつくなり重力がますと体のバランスがくずれ転がる。こうして前進する

©円谷プロ

ミイラ怪獣 ドドンゴ

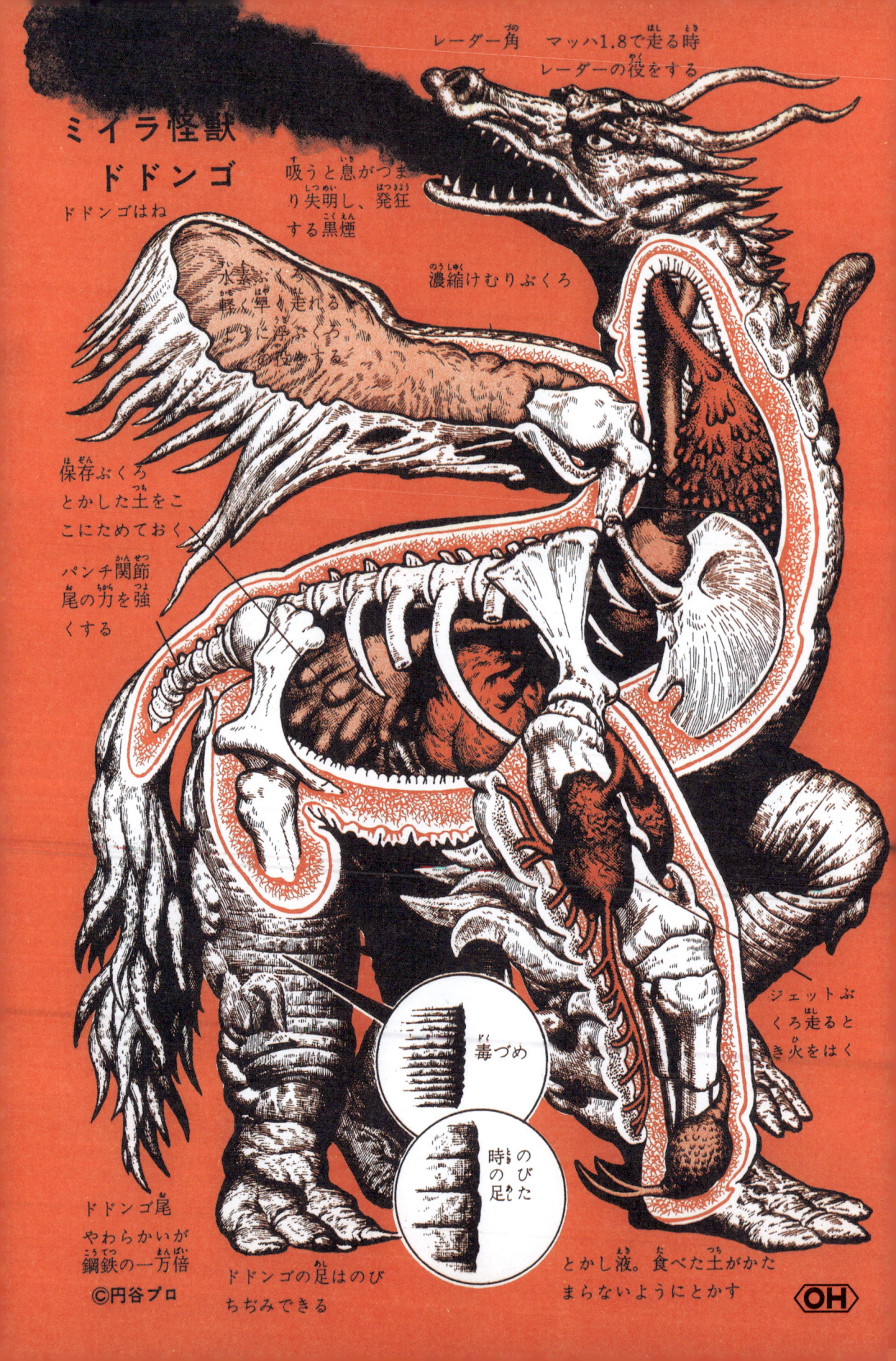

レーダー角 マッハ1.8で走る時レーダーの役をする

吸うと息がつまり失明し、発狂する黒煙

ドドンゴはね 水素ぶくろ 軽く早く走れるに浮ぶくろの役もする

濃縮けむりぶくろ

保存ぶくろ とかした土をここにためておく

パンチ関節 尾の力を強くする

ジェットぶくろ 走ると火をはく

毒づめ

のびた時の足

ドドンゴ尾 やわらかいが鋼鉄の一万倍

ドドンゴの足はのびちぢみできる

とかし液。食べた土がかたまらないようにとかす

© 円谷プロ

PAGE 81: SUBTERRANEAN TELESDON
- Eyes weak to direct sunlight
- Tapered head can bore through rock
- Epidermis 2,000 times the strength of steel
- Magma sac (just below heart)
- Brain matter divided into five sections distributed through the body: head, back, arms, and tail (he is resilient to blows to the head)
- Tail has the power of 100,000 bulldozers
- Powerful legs can topple a 30-story building
- Epidermis is 60 centimeters thick

PAGE 82: GAMERA
(Flame Kaiju Gamera)
- Gamera can see at night
- Gamera brain (at back of head)
- Flames can be thrown from hands
- Powerful hands can lift 50,000-ton ship
- Upper Abdomen: lungs and sacs for lava
- Lower Abdomen: Separate sacs for petroleum, fire, uranium, and coal
- Jet power in legs
- Tail has paralyzing poison
- Spring-coil tail is a deadly weapon

PAGE 83: GAPPA
(Giant Beast Gappa)
- Radar horn
- Rear horn is an antenna for outer space transmissions
- 4,000-degree light beam shooting from mouth and eyes can fry people
- Sensitive ears can distinguish and identify any sound
- Abdomen: Light energy sac, stomach filled with octopi
- Scales are sharp as knives
- Steel nails
- Tail strong enough to topple a building

PAGES 84–85: GYAOS
(Killer Sonic Wave Kaiju Gyaos)
- Radar ears
- Radar horns on wing tips
- Tuning fork in voice box amplifies sound to a frequency of 3 million hertz
- Poisonous nails
- One bite of its teeth can topple a building
- Yellow liquid squirting from its chest can paralyze rivals
- Abdomen: Sac holds dried, powdered version of its poison
- Juicerlike stomach extracts blood from its human food
- Two stomachs and slimy intestines

PAGES 86–87: BRETON
(Fourth Dimension Kaiju Breton)
- Protrusions contain energy-storing crystals
- During flight two whiskers shoot lasers
- Emits waves that push people into the fourth dimension
- Total length of brain channels is more than distance between Tokyo and Nagasaki
- Center: Nervous system, command function
- Outer shell is made of copper
- Shell quickly becomes thicker and heavier for balance and to prevent rolling

PAGE 88: MUMMY KAIJU DODONGO
- Radar horn
- Horn reduces draft at Mach 1.3 speed
- Breathing its black fumes leads to madness
- Throat contains a sac of concentrated fumes
- Powerful wings allow for agile midair moves
- Abdomen contains storage sacs
- Jet sacs in the legs produce fire
- Powerful tail for punching is 10,000 times stronger than steel
- Legs can extend and contract

注目獣

EYEZON

Character Design and Illustrations by Mark Nagata

Inspired by the cross sections of Shoji Ohtomo, artist Mark Nagata has rendered the interior makeup of one of his own kaiju creations, Eyezon. In contrast to the yokai, a genre of monsters mostly made up of phantoms and ghouls, kaiju have a definite corporeal existence. Their fearsome strength (however unlikely and campy it may seem at times) comes from a tangible and quantifiable reserve of biological or chemical power. All of the awesome terror that kaiju inspire in the story's protagonists and the havoc they wreak in the cities can ultimately be explained through science, albeit within the parameters of the fiction. Drawing on that idea, Nagata has provided a cross section of Eyezon, a character whose backstory is as follows: The kaiju identified as Eyezon was considered a relatively high threat as it may exist in multiples. In a failed attempt to create low-carbohydrate potato starch, scientists in Belarus (contracted by an American food tech company) conducted electron-beam irradiation experiments to study the solubility of starch in cold solutions. The inadvertent result was a transformation of energy that induced hypertrophy of the potato eyes and tubular roots, yielding a 50-meter-tall kaiju. The extent of its power is unclear, though researchers do not discount, for example, the possibility of flight. The military has been able to isolate one specimen for analysis and dissection. This kaiju was considered to be the product of exposure of normal potatoes to nuclear radiation. Further investigation, however, suggests it may be an extraterrestrial life form.

Cutaneous Layer

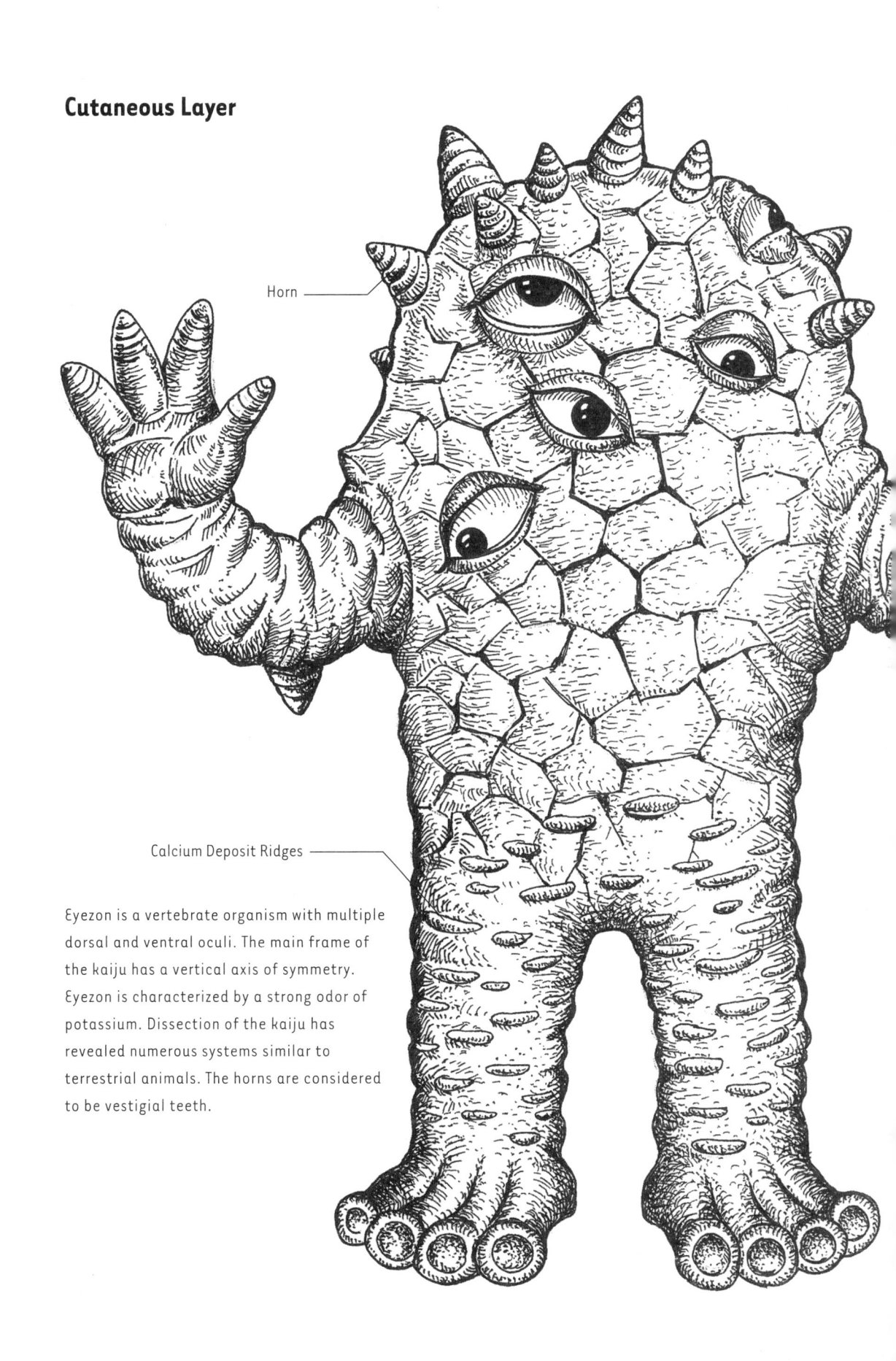

Horn

Calcium Deposit Ridges

Eyezon is a vertebrate organism with multiple dorsal and ventral oculi. The main frame of the kaiju has a vertical axis of symmetry. Eyezon is characterized by a strong odor of potassium. Dissection of the kaiju has revealed numerous systems similar to terrestrial animals. The horns are considered to be vestigial teeth.

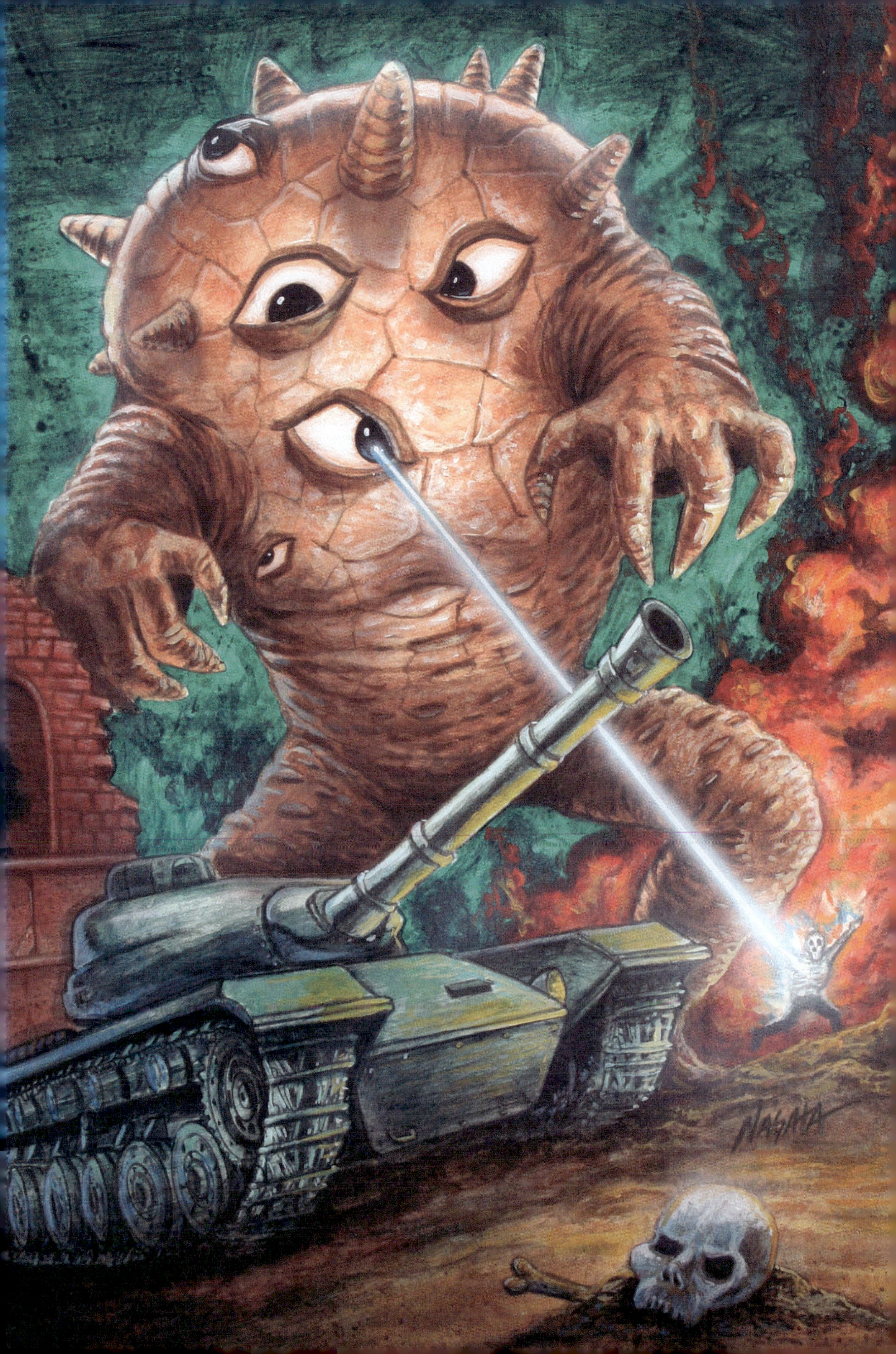

Musculature

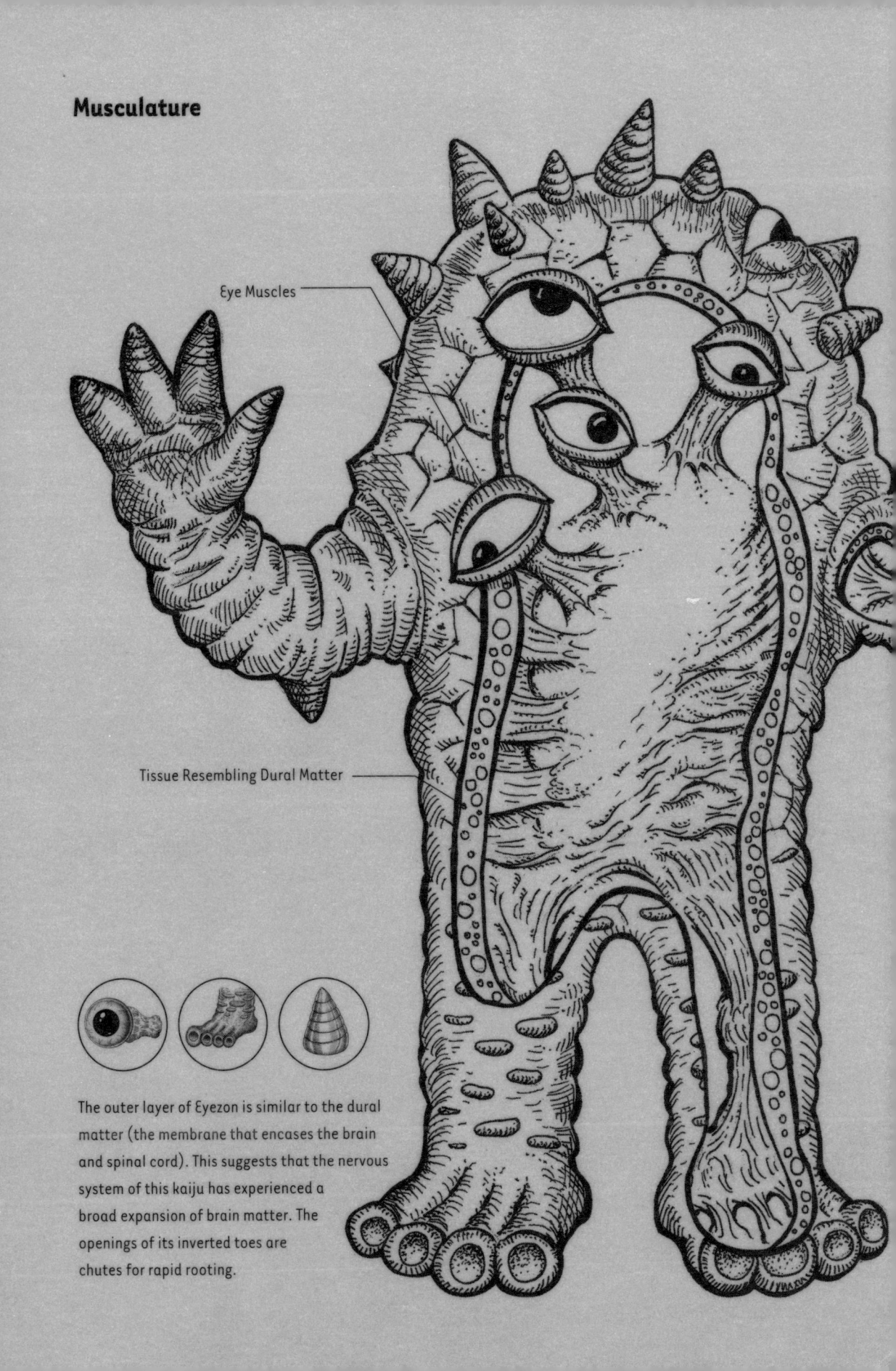

Eye Muscles

Tissue Resembling Dural Matter

The outer layer of Eyezon is similar to the dural matter (the membrane that encases the brain and spinal cord). This suggests that the nervous system of this kaiju has experienced a broad expansion of brain matter. The openings of its inverted toes are chutes for rapid rooting.

Musculature

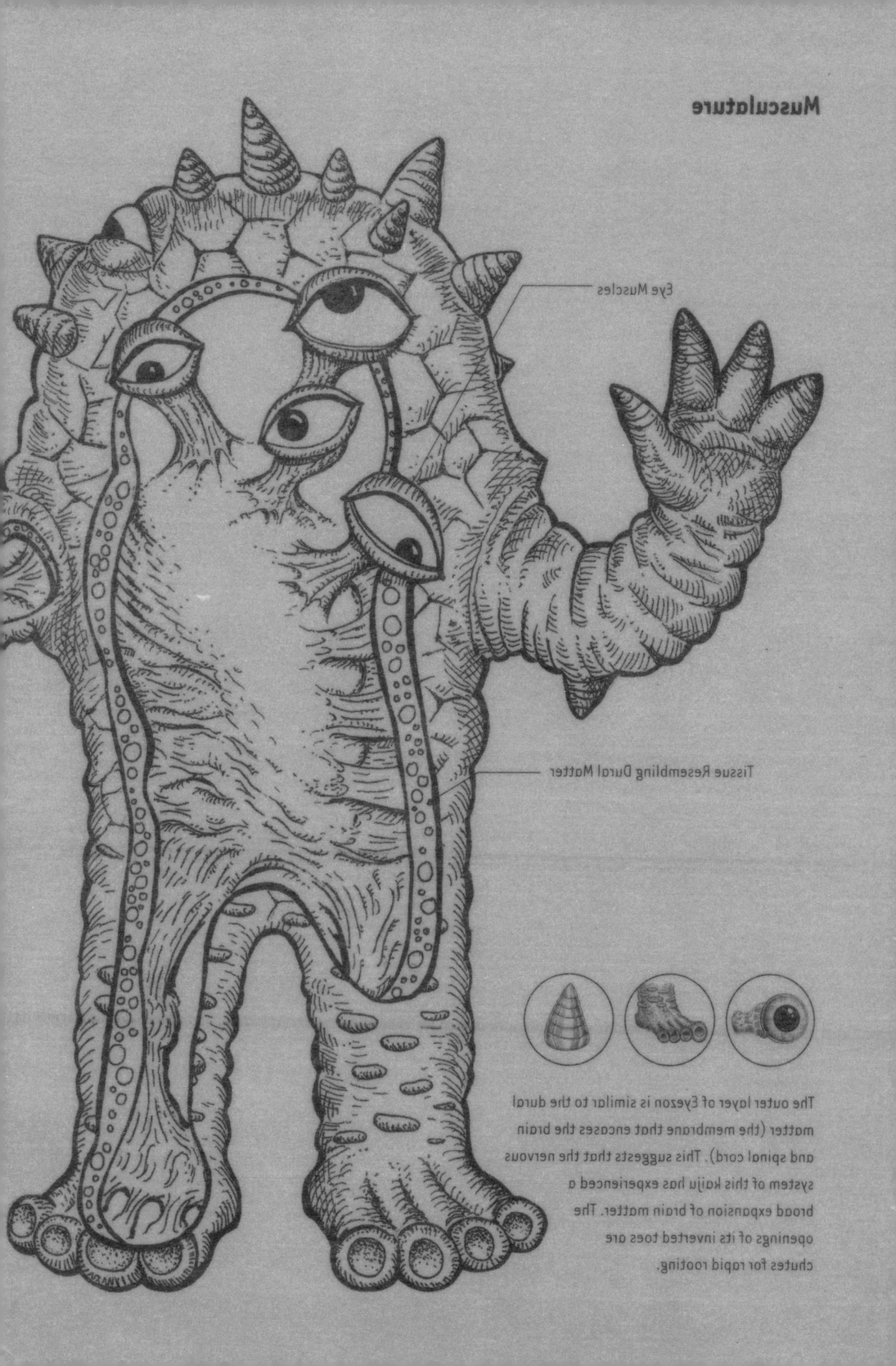

Eye Muscles

Tissue Resembling Dural Matter

The outer layer of Eyezon is similar to the dural matter (the membrane that encases the brain and spinal cord). This suggests that the nervous system of this kaiju has experienced a broad expansion of brain matter. The openings of its inverted toes are chutes for rapid rooting.

Internal Organs

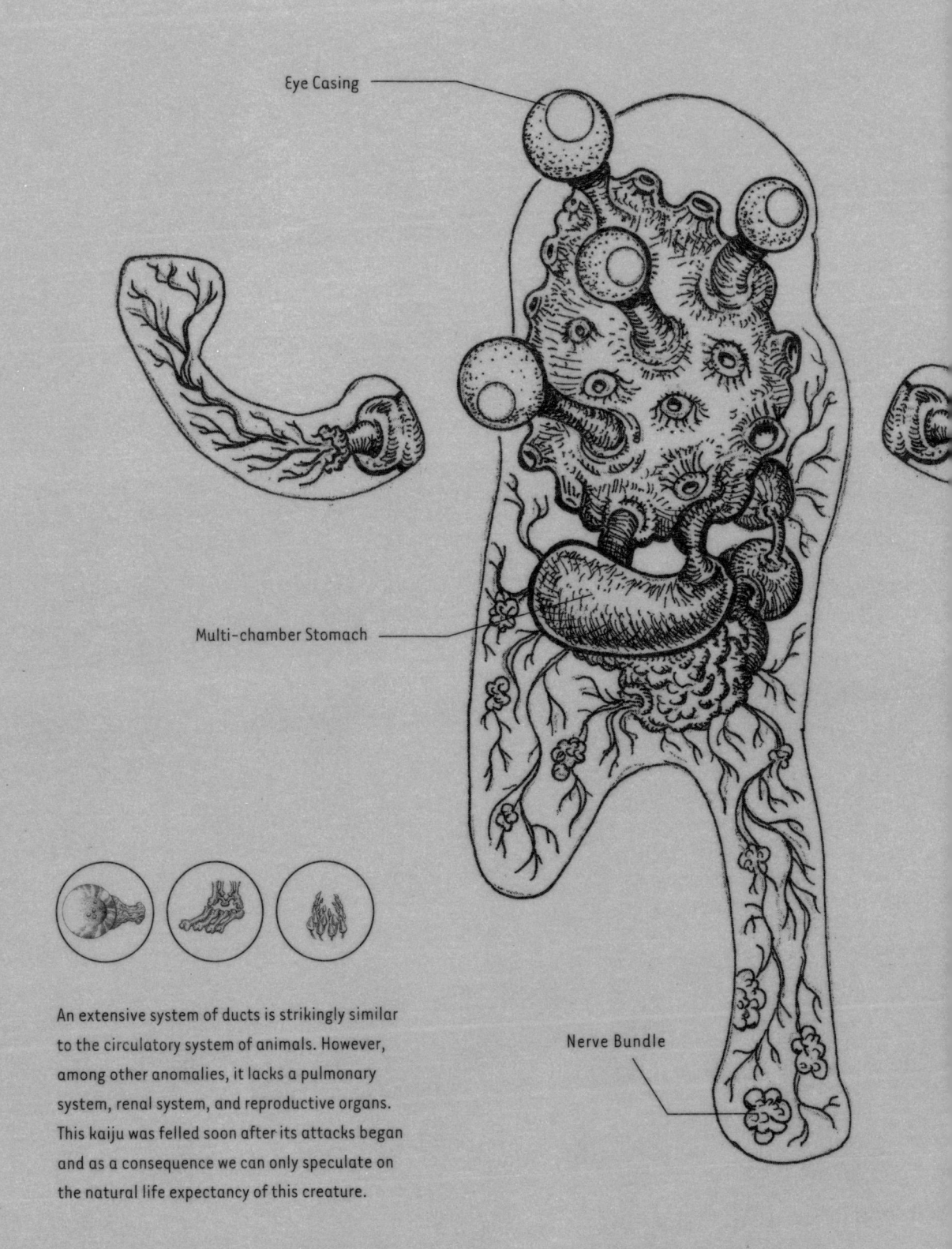

Eye Casing

Multi-chamber Stomach

Nerve Bundle

An extensive system of ducts is strikingly similar to the circulatory system of animals. However, among other anomalies, it lacks a pulmonary system, renal system, and reproductive organs. This kaiju was felled soon after its attacks began and as a consequence we can only speculate on the natural life expectancy of this creature.

Internal Organs

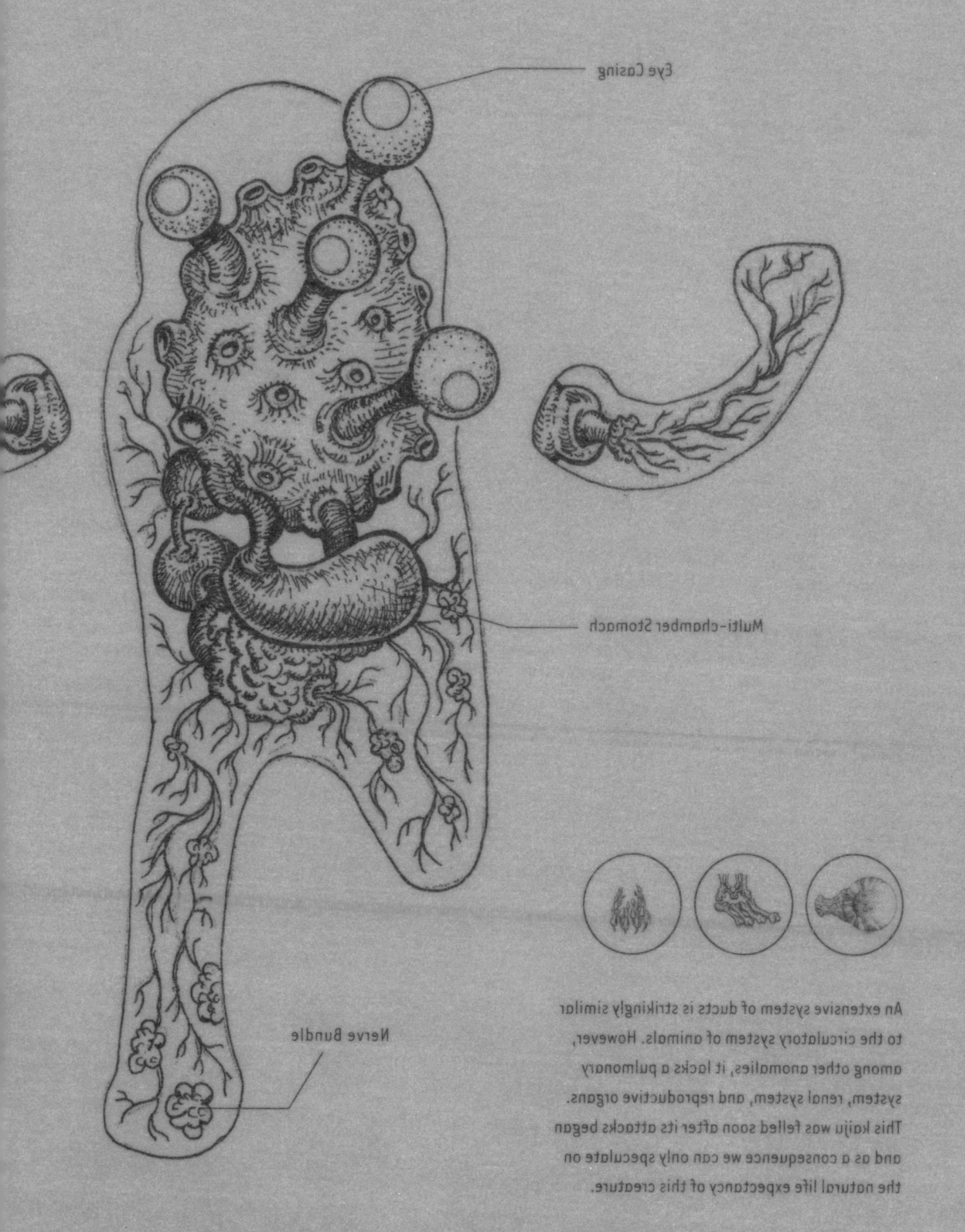

Eye Casing

Multi-chamber Stomach

Nerve Bundle

An extensive system of ducts is strikingly similar to the circulatory system of animals. However, among other anomalies, it lacks a pulmonary system, renal system, and reproductive organs. This kaiju was felled soon after its attacks began and as a consequence we can only speculate on the natural life expectancy of this creature.

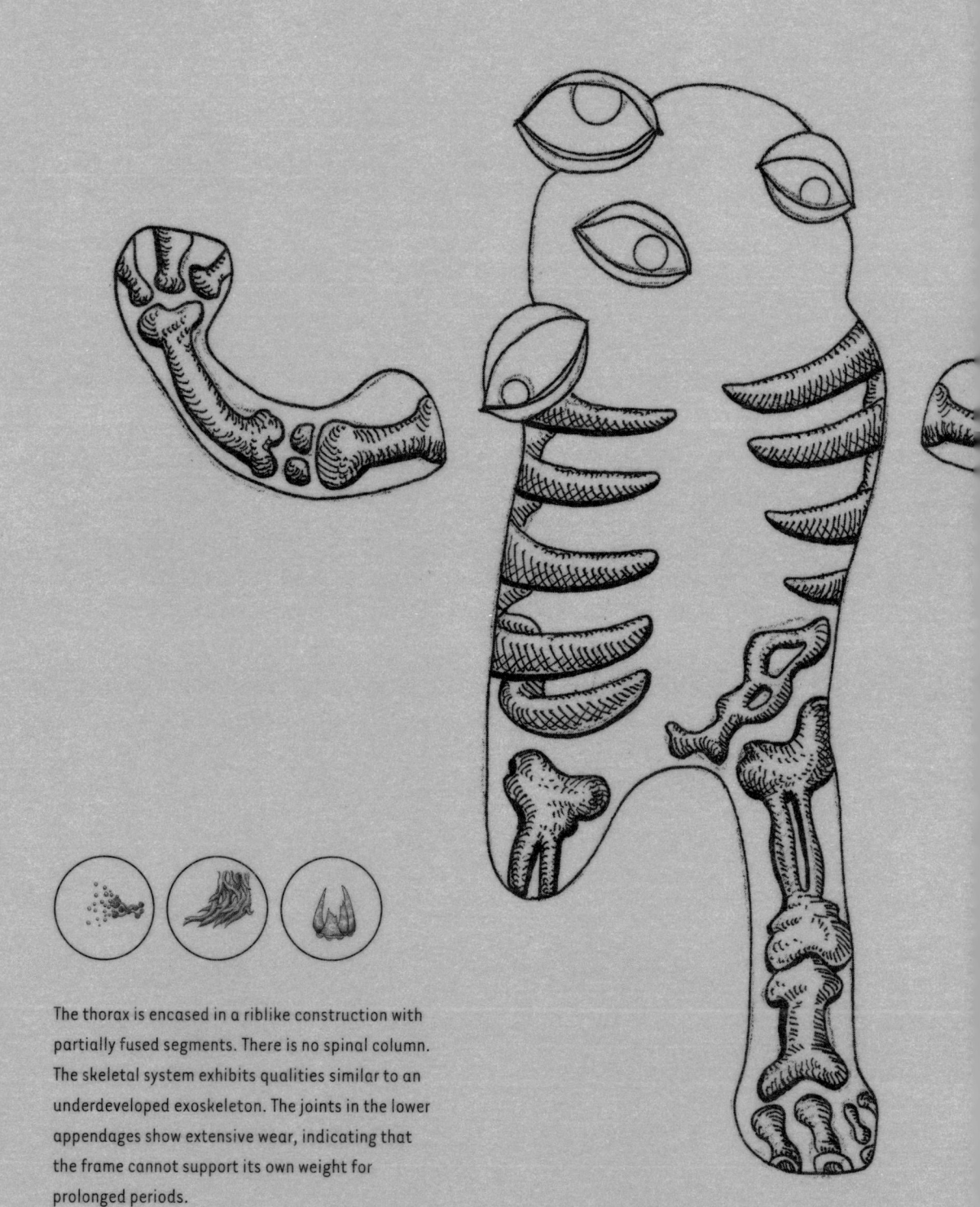

Skeletal System

The thorax is encased in a riblike construction with partially fused segments. There is no spinal column. The skeletal system exhibits qualities similar to an underdeveloped exoskeleton. The joints in the lower appendages show extensive wear, indicating that the frame cannot support its own weight for prolonged periods.

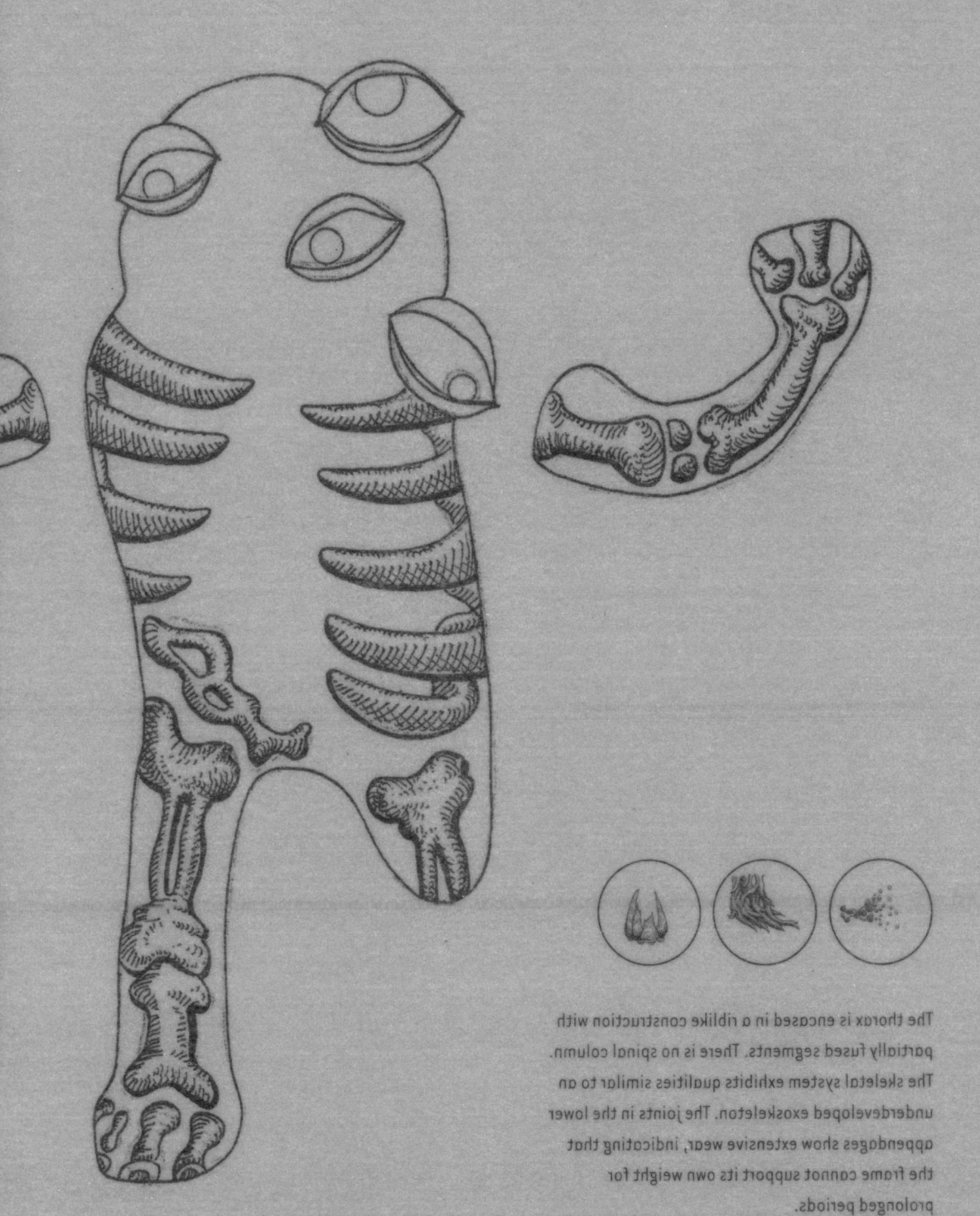

Skeletal System

The thorax is encased in a riblike construction with partially fused segments. There is no spinal column. The skeletal system exhibits qualities similar to an underdeveloped exoskeleton. The joints in the lower appendages show extensive wear, indicating that the frame cannot support its own weight for prolonged periods.

Extraspectral Dimension

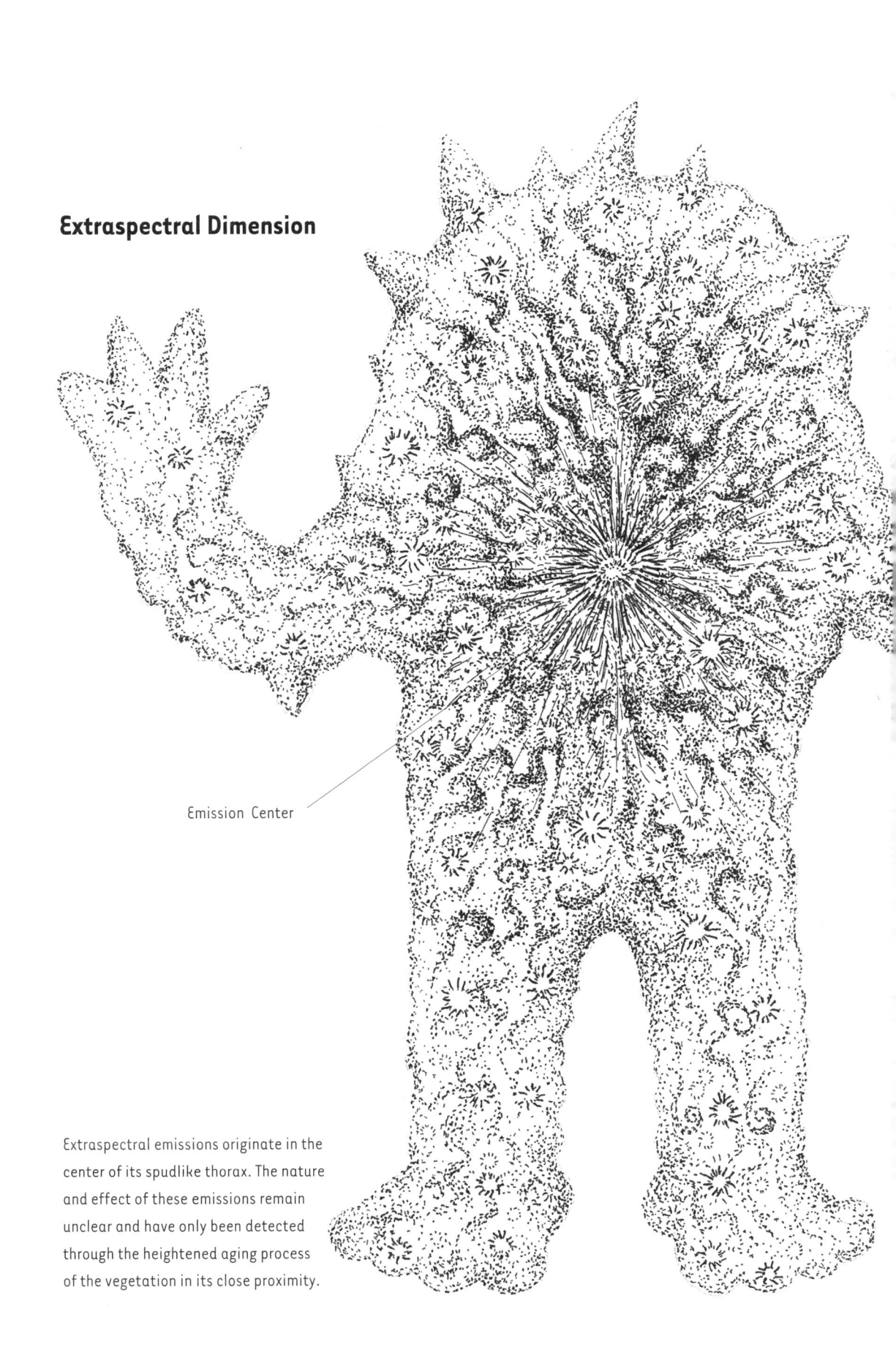

Emission Center

Extraspectral emissions originate in the center of its spudlike thorax. The nature and effect of these emissions remain unclear and have only been detected through the heightened aging process of the vegetation in its close proximity.

玩具
Soft-Vinyl Figures

Kaiju feature films of the 1950s and television productions of the 1960s and 1970s engendered an entire industry of licensed soft-vinyl toys. With a market hungry for a continuous stream of new and unique characters, several manufacturers began producing kaiju-inspired toys (with a mixture of licensed characters and the manufacturers' own originals). The initial fervor for kaiju figures was part of a larger boom in garage kit sets and plastic models. These were quite popular with a broad range of collectors and hobbyists, not just with young boys. Of the numerous kaiju figure makers, Marusan was the leader of the pack in the early years. Their lineup of Ultraman-themed toys was so popular that the maker couldn't keep up with demand. With so many manufacturers releasing competing toys at the same time, however, the market became saturated and unstable, devaluing the industry as a whole. In tandem with a temporarily waning interest in kaiju films and television shows, this was a precarious situation that soon proved untenable. The company closed its doors in 1968, but the following year most of the former employees reassembled for a new endeavor, Bullmark. This company also enjoyed a stretch of bountiful returns, thanks to a second wave of interest in all things kaiju in the 1970s. As a seal of authenticity, each of the figures was stamped on the base of the foot with their logo—a silhouette of a bull. Starting in 1973 Bullmark also made toys using die-casts, sold under the name Zinclon—a brand that included many characters from the Godzilla series. In 1977 Bullmark also went out of business. In more recent years, Bullmark's founder Saburo Ishizuki is still involved in toy production, namely with manufacturers M-1 and Bandai (who are reissuing several of the early Bullmark vinyl figures).

These figures are now highly desireable items in the secondary trade market. The demand for rare color variations, figures produced in limited production runs, or one-off items is fueled by a generation of adults who first bought the figures as youths. These figures have also inspired a new breed of kaiju toy makers who create figures in the style of the classics (as seen on pages 98–107). The figures assembled here are the products of several of these collector/creators. The means of production are such that limited runs of toys can be manufactured employing a relatively sensible economic model. M-1, Max Toys, Toy Graph, Dream Rockets, and Target Earth are contemporary toy makers who accurately create original figures in the tradition of Marusan and Bullmark. The mini-figure was also a common item of this period, and is a style emulated by Dokuro Taro (page 103).

Pages 95–97: Vintage toys from the collection of Shuji Kajimoto, the proprietor of Toy Graph. **Opposite:** A mixture of Marusan and Bullmark figures based on Tsuburaya characters, including multiple Ultraman figures in various sizes.

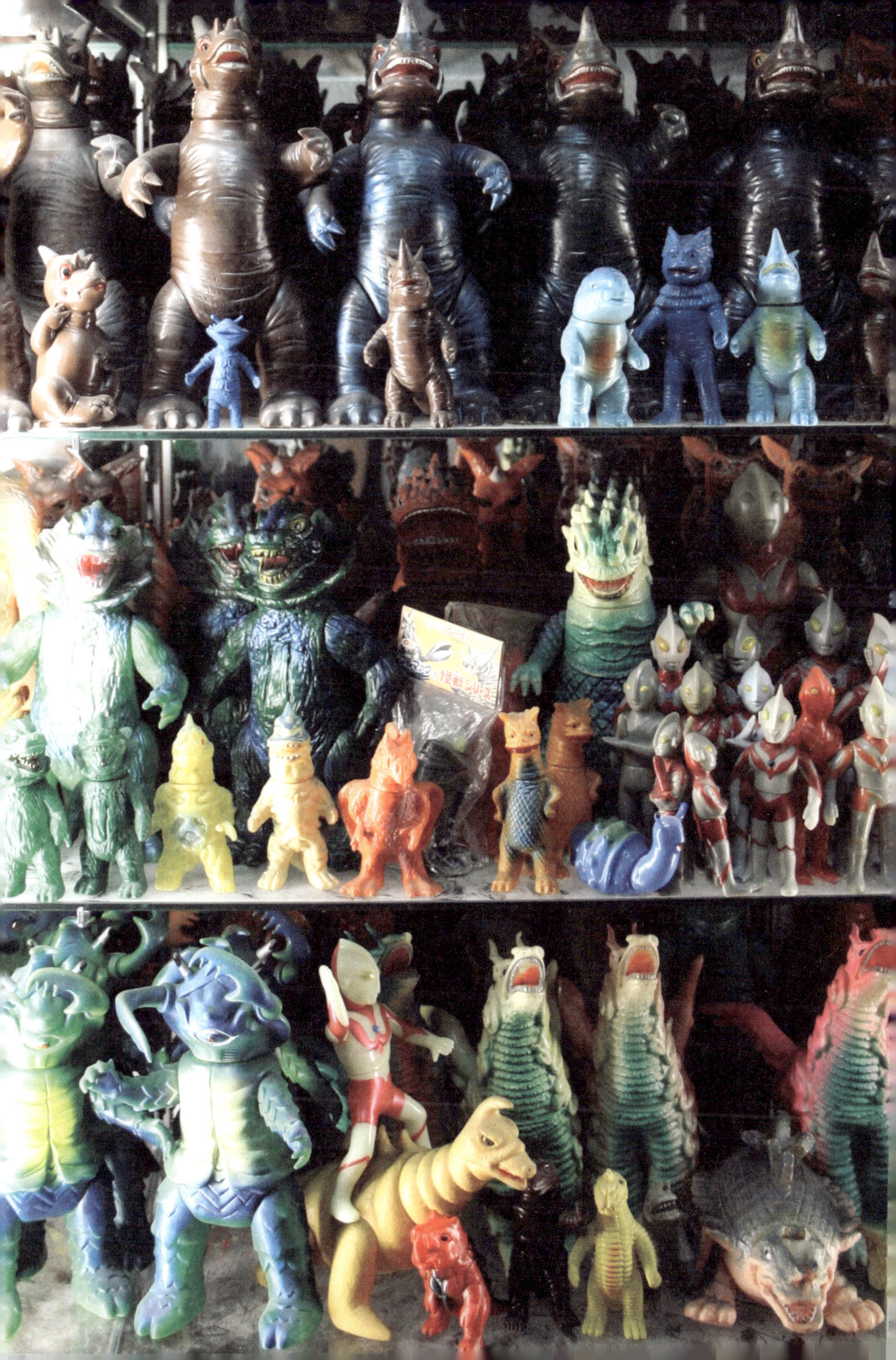

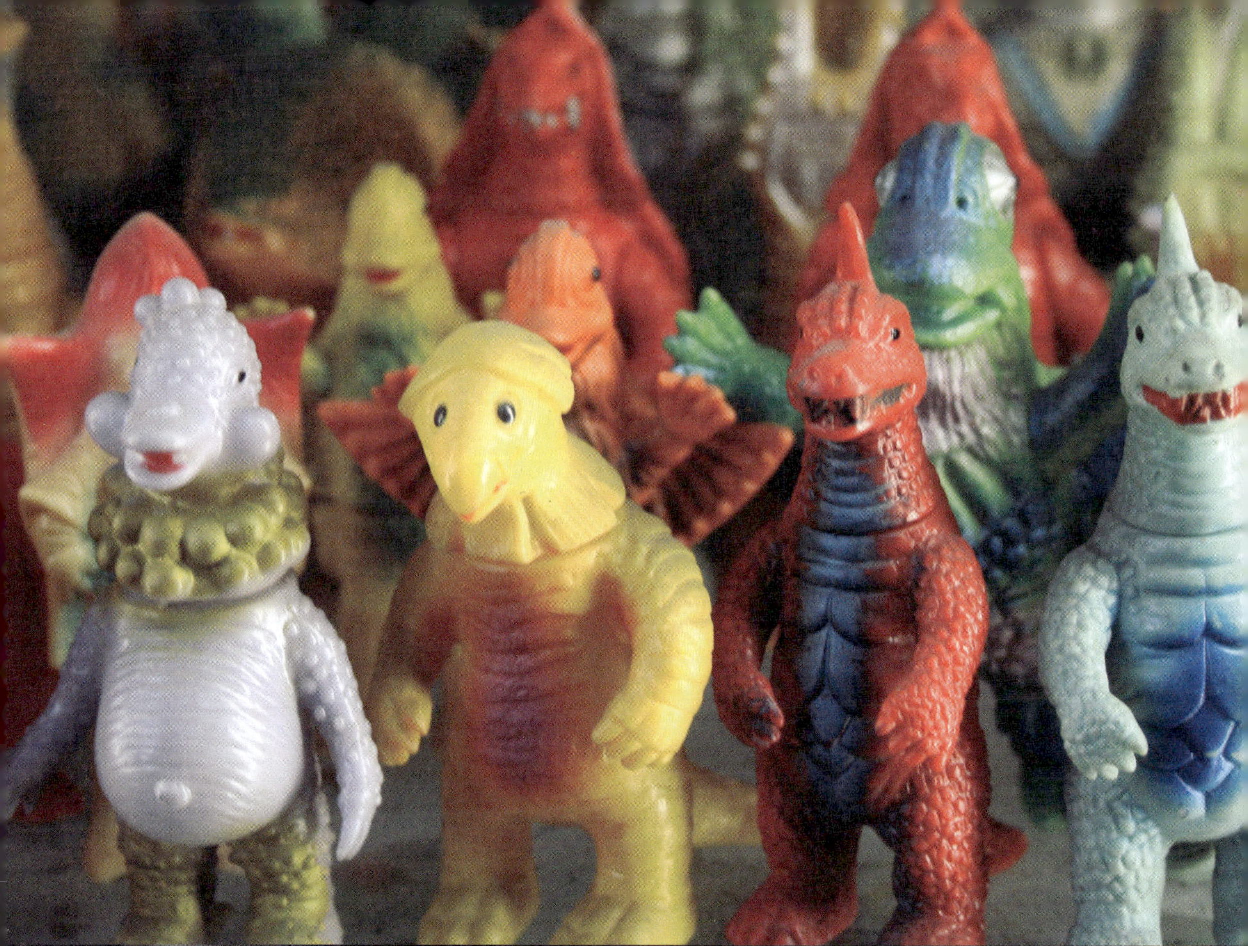
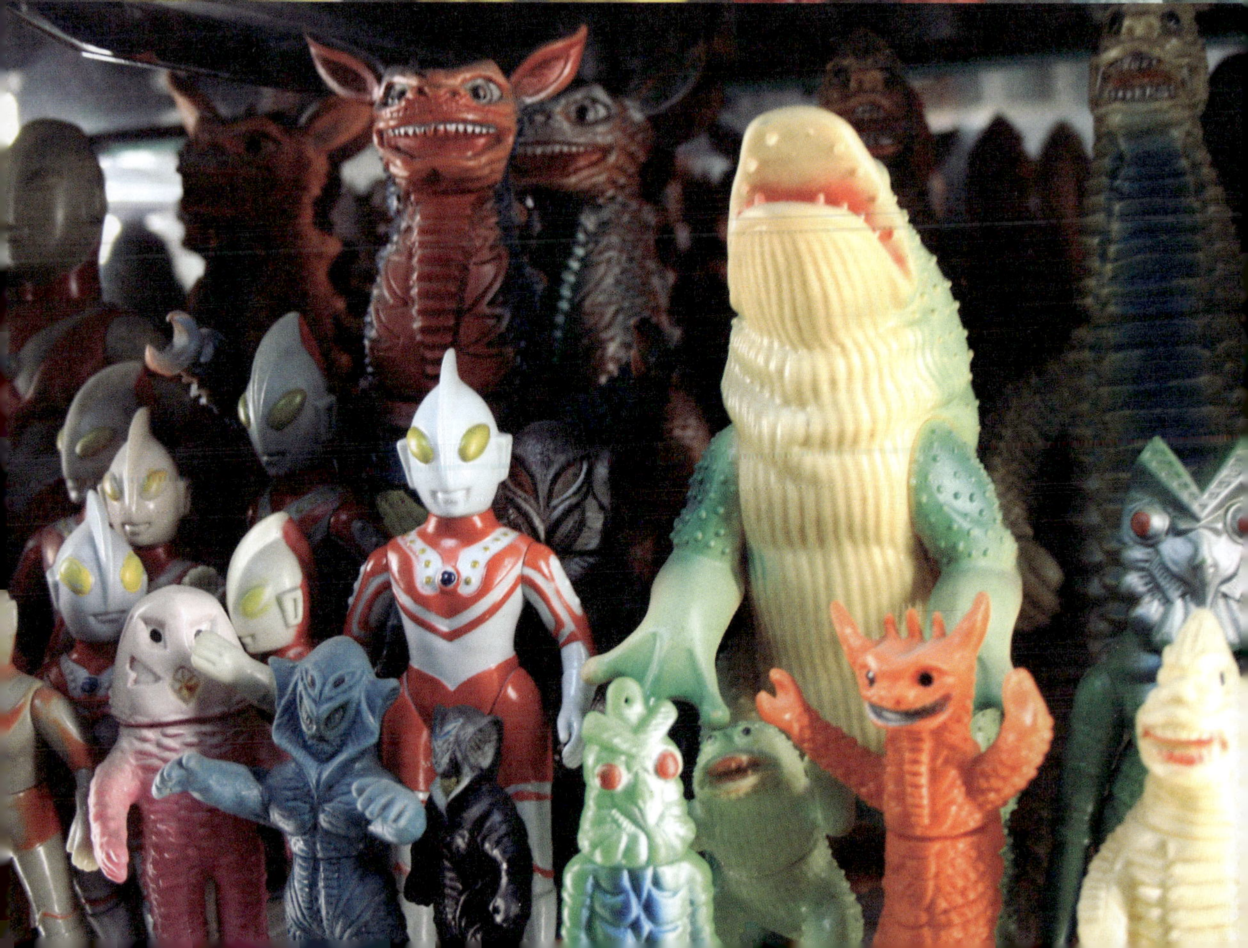

This spread: Marusan and Bullmark miniature figures. Early toys were closer in shape to Kewpie. The legs and lower half of the figure helped stabilize the form.

Figures by MAX TOYS

Tripus ▼

This three-tentacled octopus is a sea-dwelling diety and protects long-buried dominions. It emerges to the surface in vengeful attacks on the humans who have polluted the sea's waters with nuclear testing.

Alien Xam ▲

Alien Xam is the arch nemesis to Captain Max. Their ultimate conflict is not a battle of brute power but rather a contest between good and evil. As their names infer (one is a reverse of the other), they are inextricably linked.

Booska ▶

Booska is a friendly, domesticated kaiju. The figure's design (by Martin Ontiveros) is an interpretation of the original Tsuburaya Production character. The television series was broadcast from 1966 to 1967.

099

Figures by DREAM ROCKETS

Maron

Deep Earth Kaiju Gazlar

Insect Kaiju Gumoz

Figure by
DREAM ROCKETS

Fish Kaiju
Gimos

Figures by DOKURO TARO

Zunougon ▼

Zunougon is a genius kaiju. It was originally the brain of a young boy that developed a superhuman capacity. The organ developed a musculature that allowed it to function independently of its host. It also transmits telepathic waves. The brain eventually melded with a kaiju, becoming Zunougon. It takes revenge on bullies.

Honegon ▲

Honegon are a group that live somewhere near the center of the earth. They are a mysterious kaiju that come up to the surface to hunt for the brains and corpses of Zunougon.

Missilasu ▼

Missilasu is a kaiju from an unnamed country. The creature has melded with nuclear warheads.

▲ Mimigirasu

Mimigirasu has the ability to make the ears of its victims fall off. It then collects the ears to create the ultimate ear—Mimigirasu's gigantic Ear Wing.

Figures by
TARGET EARTH

Evil Dragon
Gamerudon

This kaiju has little or no intelligence and is simply driven by the impulse to destroy. It attacks whatever comes into its line of sight, regardless of what it may be. Gamerudon uses its tongue to ensnare people. Its saliva is highly acidic and can melt anything. But its tongue is also its weakness, for if it can be ripped out Gamerudon will die.

Demon Mad Cow
Faceless Bull

This kaiju appeared in a dream to a young boy. The boy's family had gone for *yakiniku* (barbecued beef) that evening, and while there he remembers a news story about a group protesting whaling. The faceless beast in his dream represents the reduction of animals to mere meat for consumption. Its head may be an exposed brain. From that day forward, the boy was a committed vegetarian.

Kogai Kaiju
Gebora

First spotted by a father and son fishing near the breakwaters of Tokyo Harbor, Gebora is an amphibious kaiju. Below its two bulging eyes, Gebora's mouth discharges liquid waste. It belches up a pitch-like liquid onto small boats, making them dissolve and disappear beneath the waves.

Figures by TOY GRAPH

The Space Troopers, from the solar system of the Ark Galaxy, are a military corps loyal to a ruling planetary alliance. The Troopers invade planets not belonging to the alliance and mine whatever energy deposits they find. Such plundering has eliminated a countless number of planets from the galaxy. The planetary alliance of the Ark Galaxy is ruled by the Dark God Zua, a preternaturally intelligent humanoid who has lived for over a thousand years. **Death 13** has excellent battle skills. He seems to be in a class above Captain, but even among the military any information about him is top secret. He is under direct orders from the Dark God Zua and active in all battles in the galaxy. Any attack from him results in death. Even the other Space Troopers fear him. **AZ Captain** is a warmonger. When planning military operations, he does not hesitate to put those under his command in peril in order to successfully complete a mission. AZ Captain is a particularly intelligent and sturdy example of the AZ-type clones and is an elite officer. When promoted to captain, he underwent surgery to strengthen himself and improve his skills. The Captain class of Space Troopers have genetic bombs stored within their bodies. Each **AZ** is one iteration of a clone breed. Like the other copies, he has a self-composed and individual character. This clone is a legendary warrior. Sixty percent of the Space Troopers are AZs. All Space Troopers have received cyborg surgery to allow them to function in space. They originate in the clone factory on the planet Raidar. **VX** is a scientist with an IQ exceeding 1,000. All the weapons used by the Space Troopers were developed by his kind. The VX belong to the same race as the Dark God Zua. They are devoid of emotions except for a sadistic pleasure in carrying out experiments on people. Members of the ruling class of the planetary alliance, they have a very long life expectancy. The only one among them with two eyes is the Dark God Zua. All others have their left eye removed in an act of allegiance at a coming-of-age ceremony. The VX are from the planet Yabou. **Mizaru-1** (design and character setting by Mark Nagata) is the half-breed offspring of an ape and an invincible alien. One part of his brain is controlled by a computer. Mizaru-1 likes to use a raygun but is particularly skilled at direct combat, utilizing hands and feet. He will also bite the flesh of opponents with his sharp teeth. Planet A.P.E. (Alien Primate Empire) is his planet of origin.

Death 13

VX

AZ Captain

Mizaru-1

AZ

怪獣切絵

Cut Drawing

by Ryohei Tanaka

A motif common to kaiju graphics of the 1950s to 1970s is silhouetted kaiju forms arranged in a monochromatic frieze. The opening sequences of the television series *Ultraman* regularly employed this technique. One of the defining characteristics of kaiju design is a distinction of form, as production companies focused primarily on warping the shapes of dinosaurs, insects, and reptiles. Such forms were combined with known animal shapes, for instance, or dispensed entirely with all plausibility. Such experiments in design yielded such kaiju as a nebulous mass of bubbles or an extremely wooly variety that lacked any distinct posterior or anterior. But the tastes of fans leaned toward the conservative. It's for this reason that many of the most beloved (and successful) kaiju characters are readily identifiable in silhouette and the most prevalent form that found favor among audiences was the biped. (Incidentally, the two-legged suit also afforded greater movement for the costumed actors while portraying one-on-one combat.) Inspired by the murals of Shigeru Matsuzaki, artist Ryohei Tanaka has created a panorama cut from a single piece of paper. The paper is folded in half at the start of the production so that the finished composition is comprised of two halves that are a mirror of one another. The final size of the cut drawing was over one meter in length. The following narrative elaborates on the possibility of the existence of a single kaiju godhead.

In the years subsequent to the apocalypse, unanswered questions were innumerable. Would the kaiju return to destroy what man had rebuilt? How many more of these kaiju could there be? Where did they come from? The surviving tribes tell the stories of this bleak period in their collective histories. There were undeniable episodes of heroism, but the overwhelming onslaught of these savage attacks has decimated their civilizations. Some believe these beasts to be more than the scaly flesh and gnashing teeth that are visible with the naked eye. There are rumors that there exists a kaiju godhead, to whom the monsters pledge unending allegiance and who has directed this attack on earth. The godhead's visage is depicted in many of the survivor's tribal crafts, most commonly shown as a fire-breathing head hovering in midair. Some depictions show a dizzying and disorienting vision—a rapidly flickering image flipping back and forth between light and dark with the ability to mesmerize all who look upon it. Many tribes impart a totemic value to the representation of the godhead and its many kaiju minions. The motif of symmetry and distinct silhouette is an imaginative depiction of this vision of the godhead. As a testament to the widespread belief in this image and of its power as a sort of talisman, most sections of the rebuilt territories are painted in a similarly monochromatic manner.

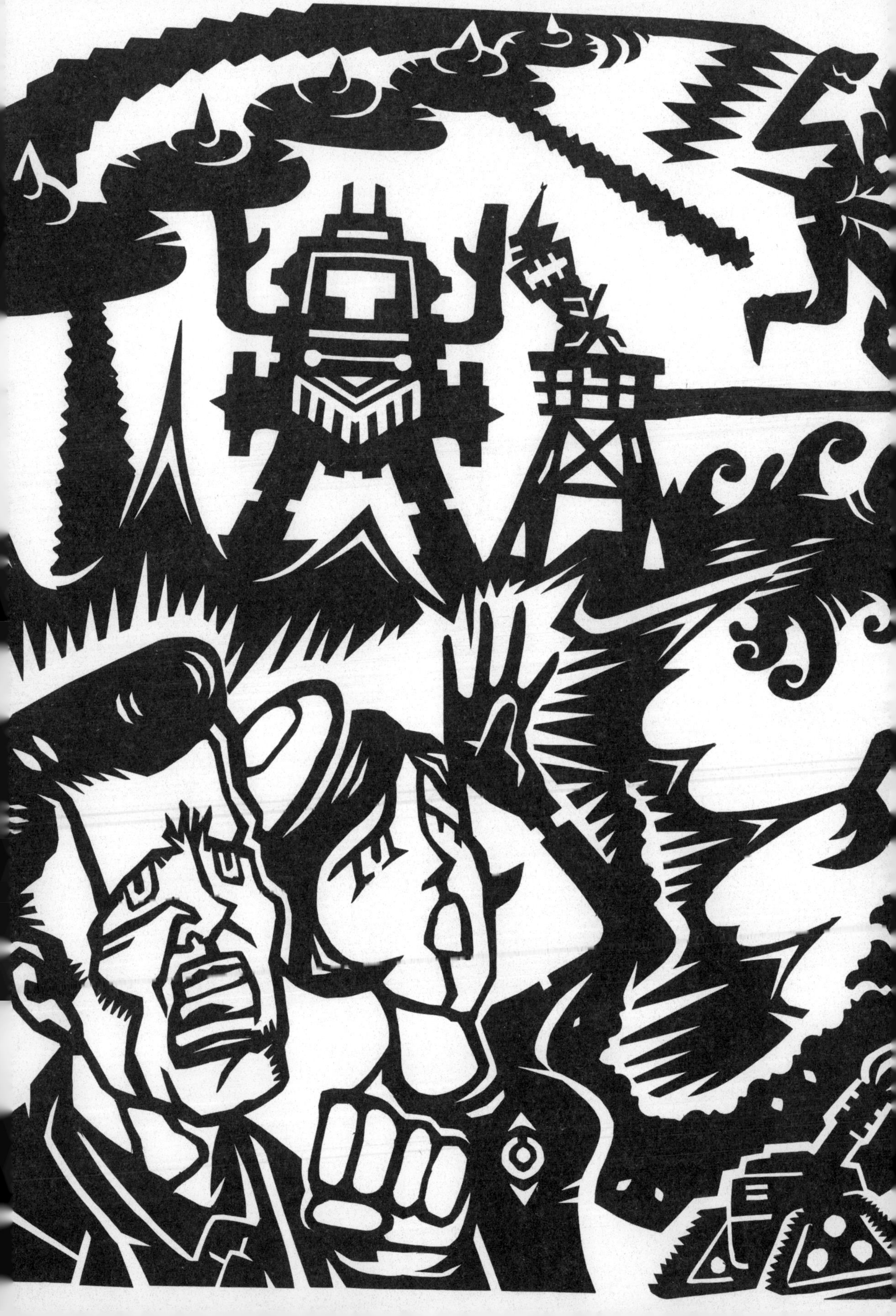

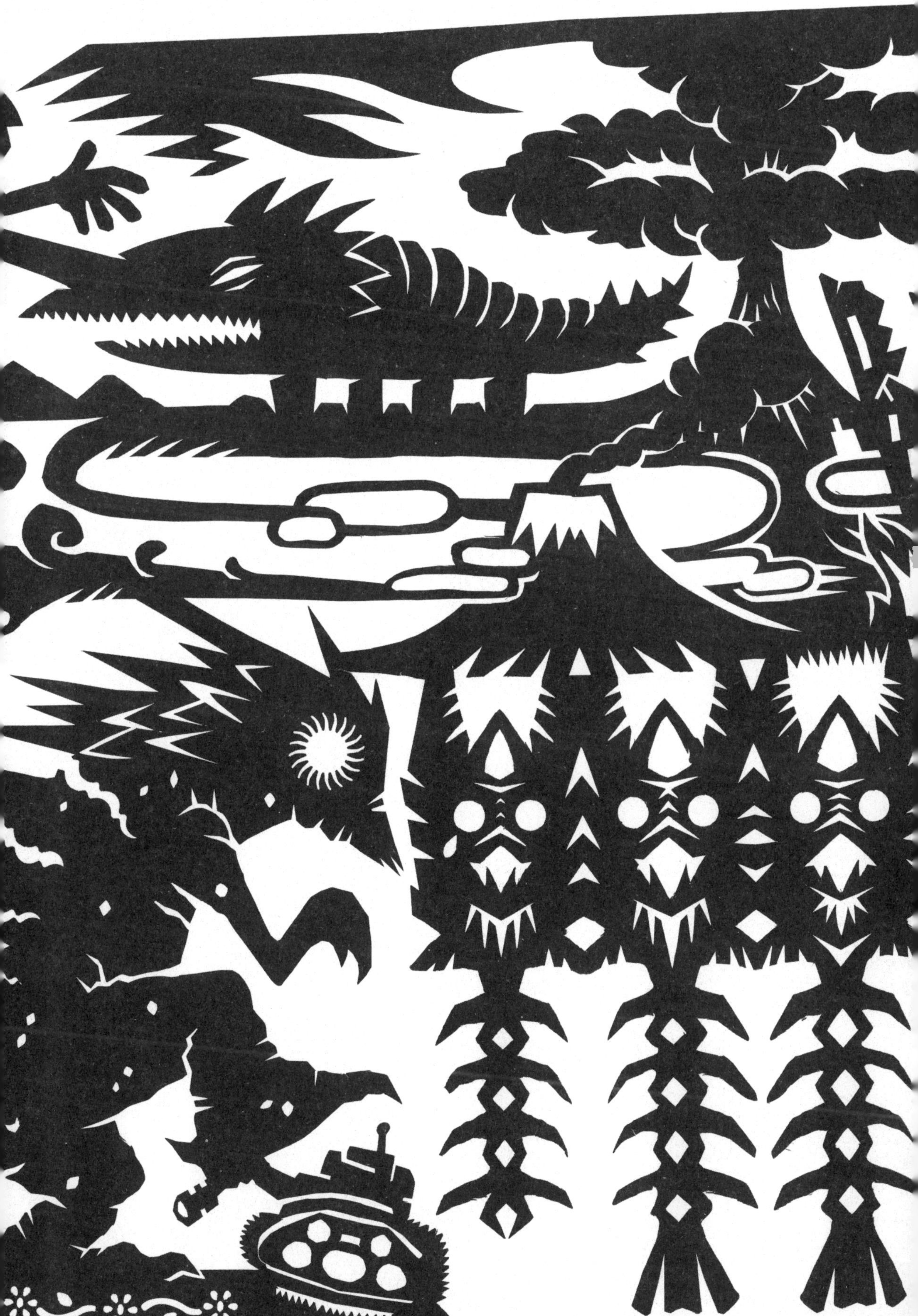

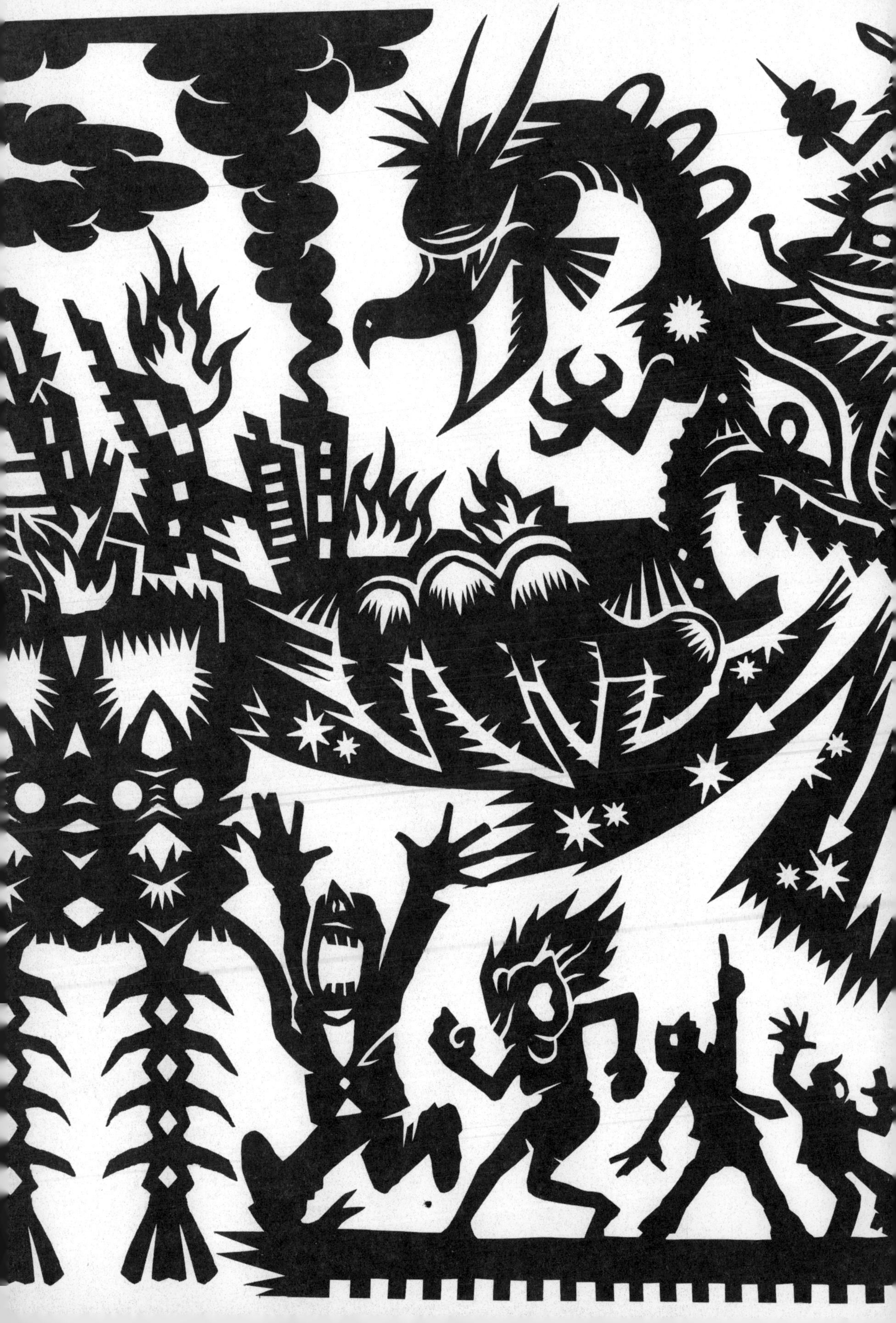

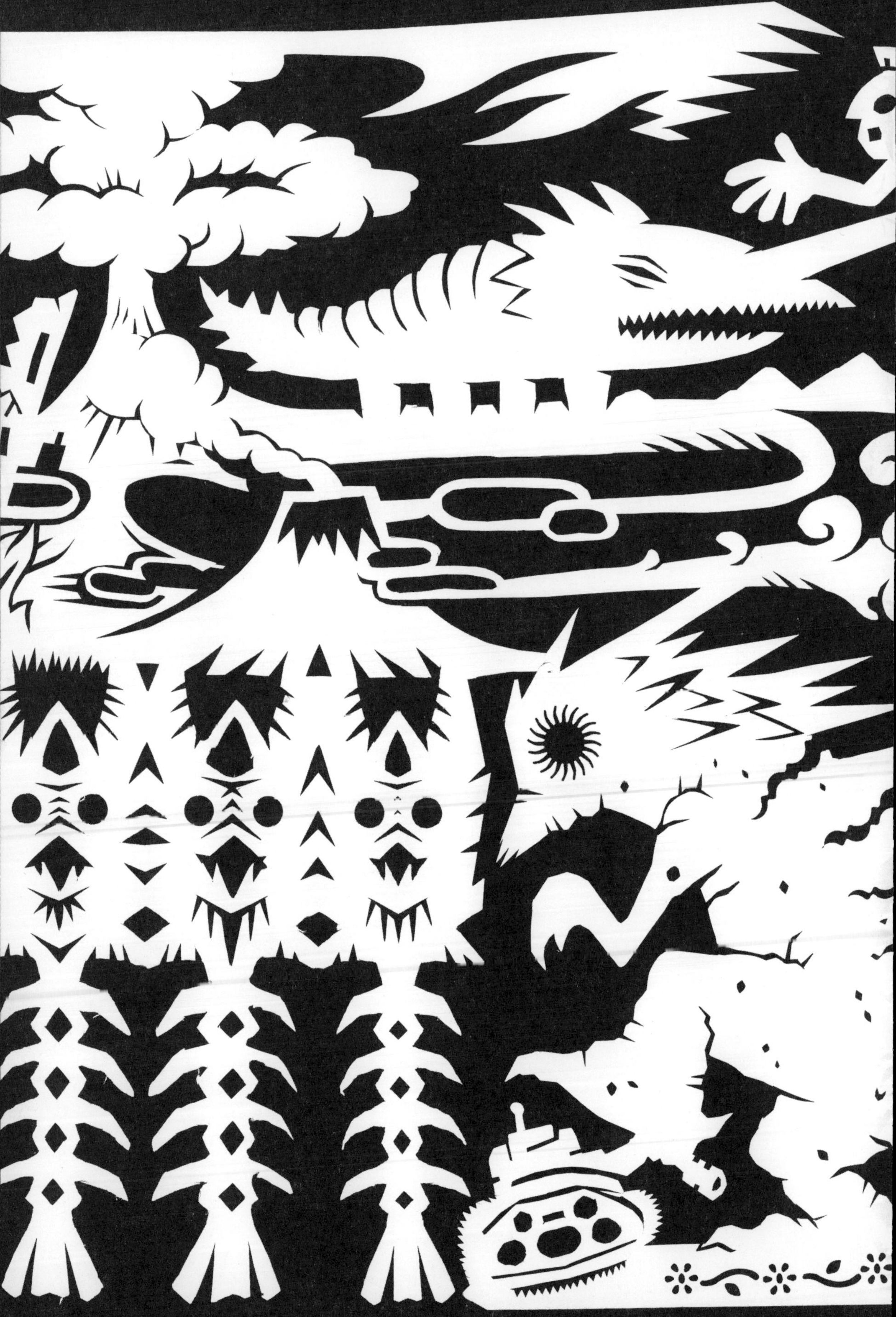

怪獣図画
Kaiju Illustration

Kaiju film and television broadcasts of the 1960s and 1970s inspired a thriving industry of printed matter (such as children's books, manga, magazines, illustrated encylopedias, and various other emphemera). The illustrations of masters such as Tohl Narita, Shigeru Komatsuzaki, Noritsuna Maemura, and Takashi Minamimura has influenced a whole generation of young people in Japan, leaving a vibrant legacy evident in the work of the contemporary artists included in this section. Classic motifs like underwater creatures, morphed figures, and the fusion of organic and inorganic matter are still prevalent in these illustrations.

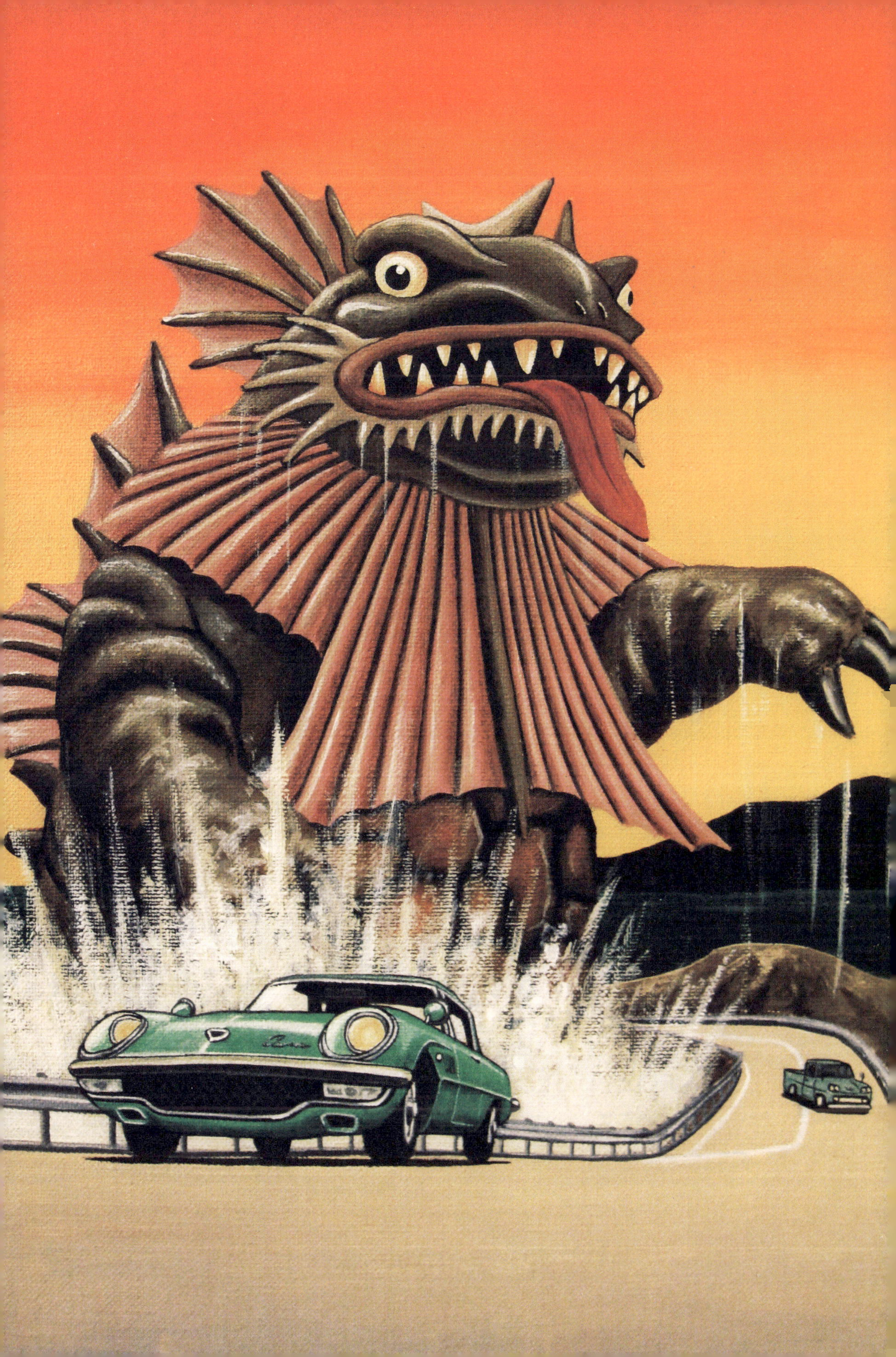

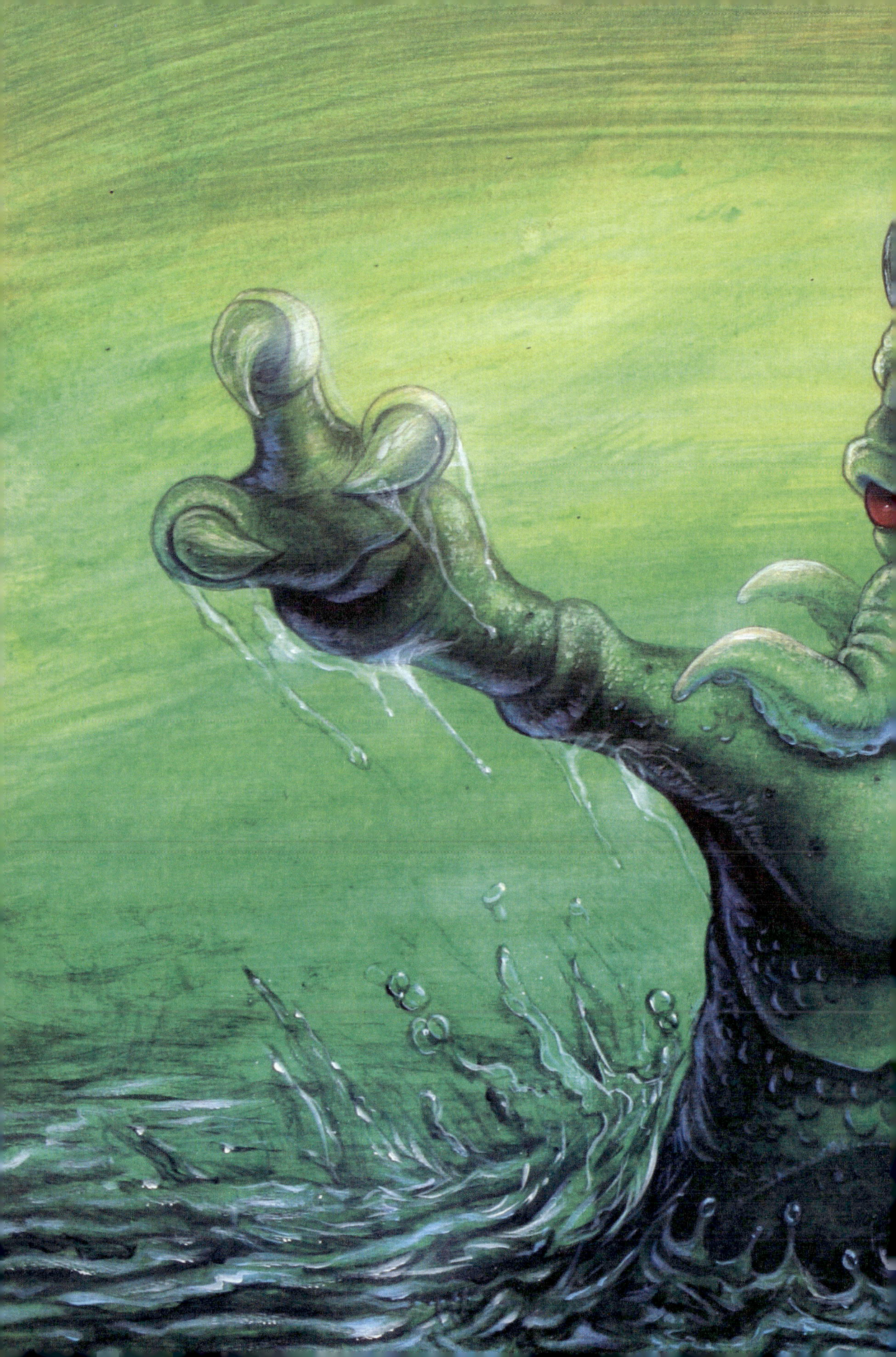

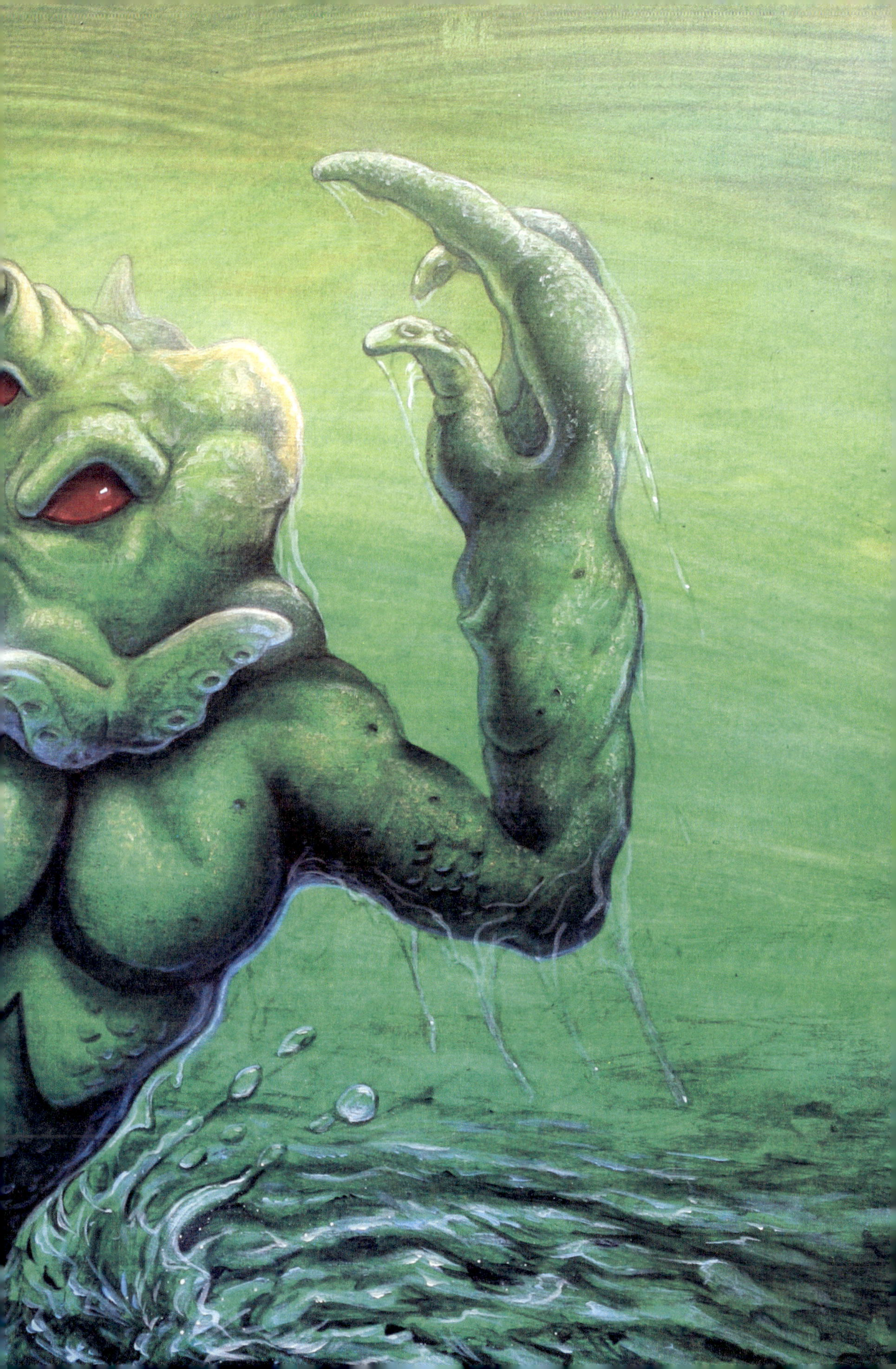

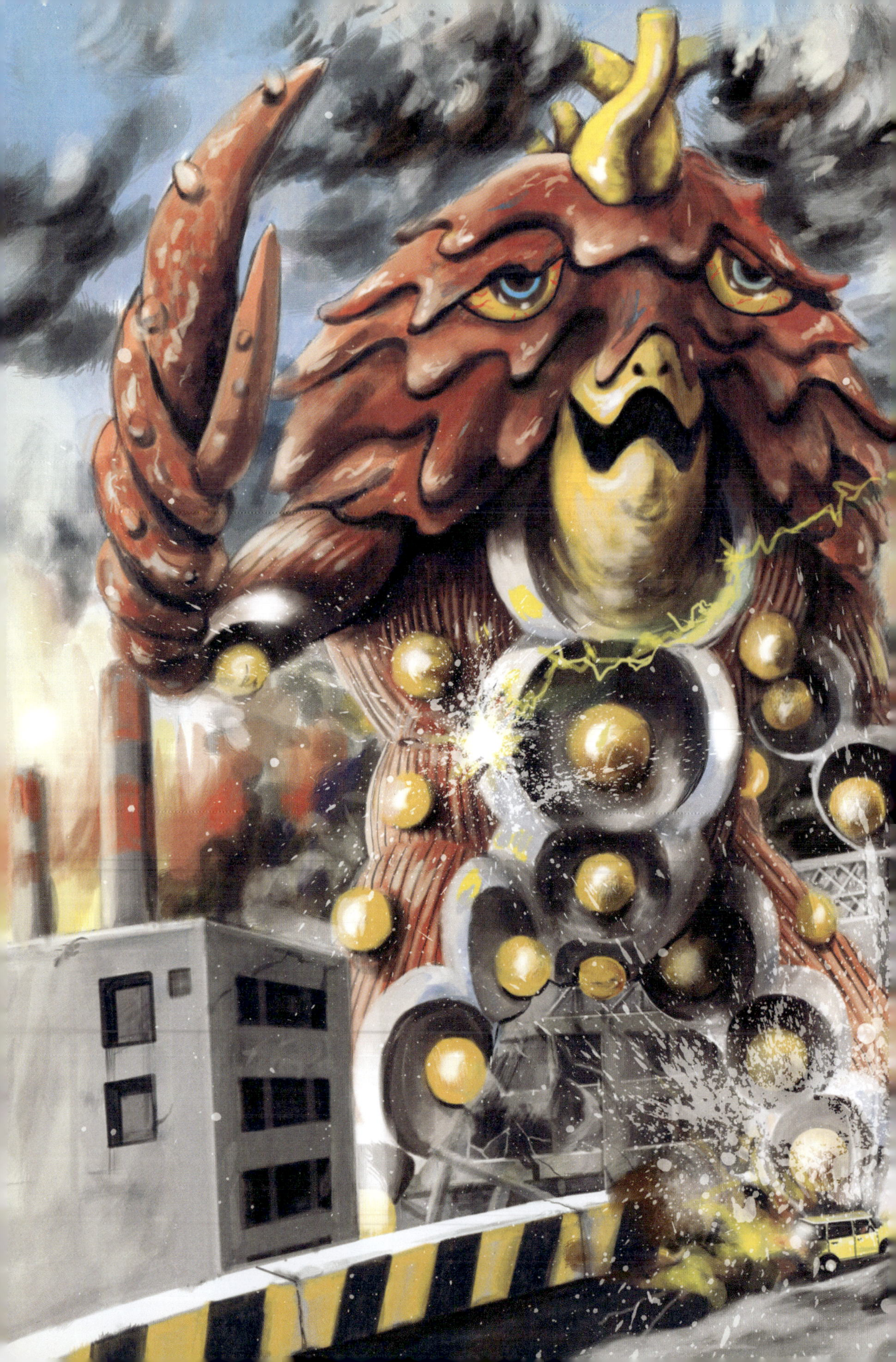

Previous spread: Tripus, a guardian deity of an aquatic kingdom, by Mark Nagata. **Opposite:** Two paintings by Imiri Sakabashira depicting giant kaiju invading cities. The retro television set of the 1960s also shows a scene typical of programs aired at that time. The small-town, neighborhood shops selling fruit and tofu is a typical Japanese image. At the same time, the sports car speeding down a mountain road represents the fantasy world preoccupation typical of young boys.

Pages 120–121: Kussai is born in the sludge of an industrial plant. It is an amalgam of crab, fish, and bird morphed together with a kaiju. Kussai aims to take revenge on humankind through its powerful telepathic capabilities. It attacks factories with fumes, smog, and sonic output from the speakers in its belly.

Pages 122–124: Crazy Mekaos (left) is a kaiju that has melded with contemporary weapons. The pilot has fallen victim to parasitical mind control. Jomera (center) is a neurosis-inducing kaiju and drives people crazy with its eyebeams. Osaka-munashi (right) is the kaiju form of the deep-seated grudge buried in Osaka.

Page 125: Numekin is a gigantic goldfish created from the unchecked excesses of biotechnological research. It melded with a kaiju from "kaiju hell," redoubled the power of its muscles, and grew horns and teeth. Numekin hates humankind's scientifically enhanced civilization and begins an attack on Tokyo.

Pages 126–127: Pekepeke Munashi is a cross between the kaiju Ghost Munashi (who hails from "kaiju hell") and the embodiment of pure, seething hatred of all townspeople. Oil paint drips from its mouth and the creature shoots flames of bitterness. Pekepeke's story, after all, is that of the misunderstood avant-garde artist.

Illustrations by Dokuro Taro

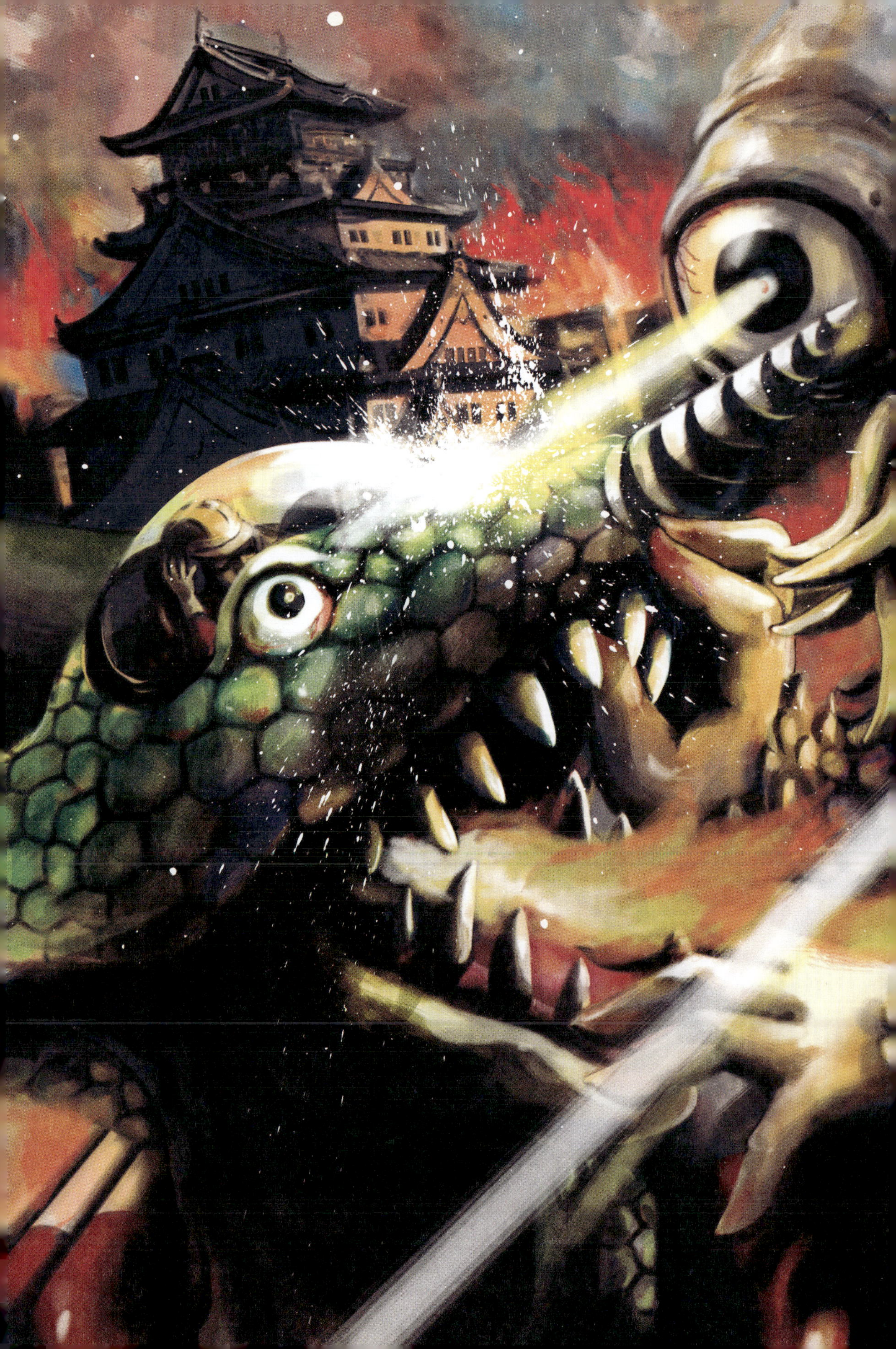

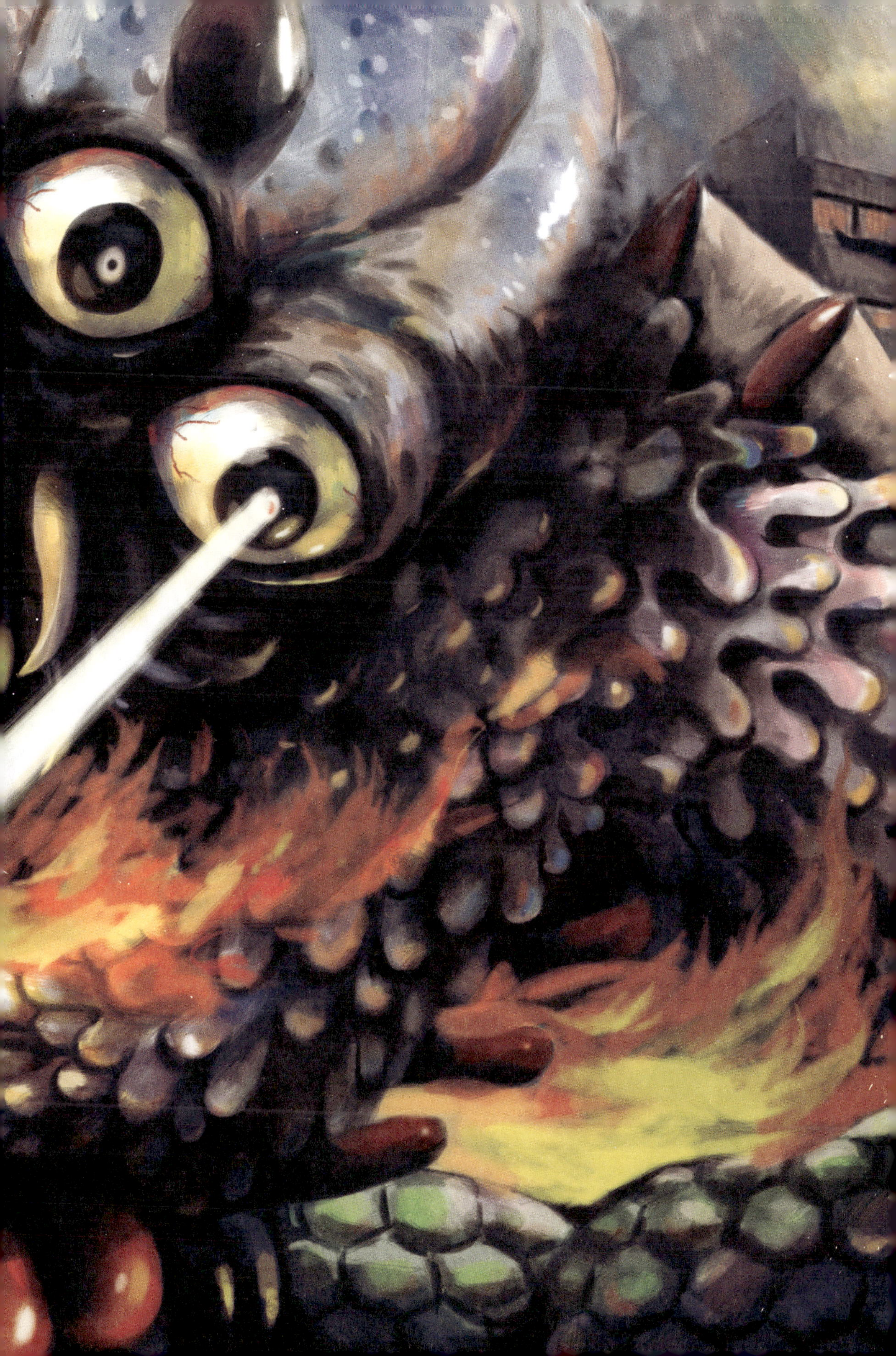

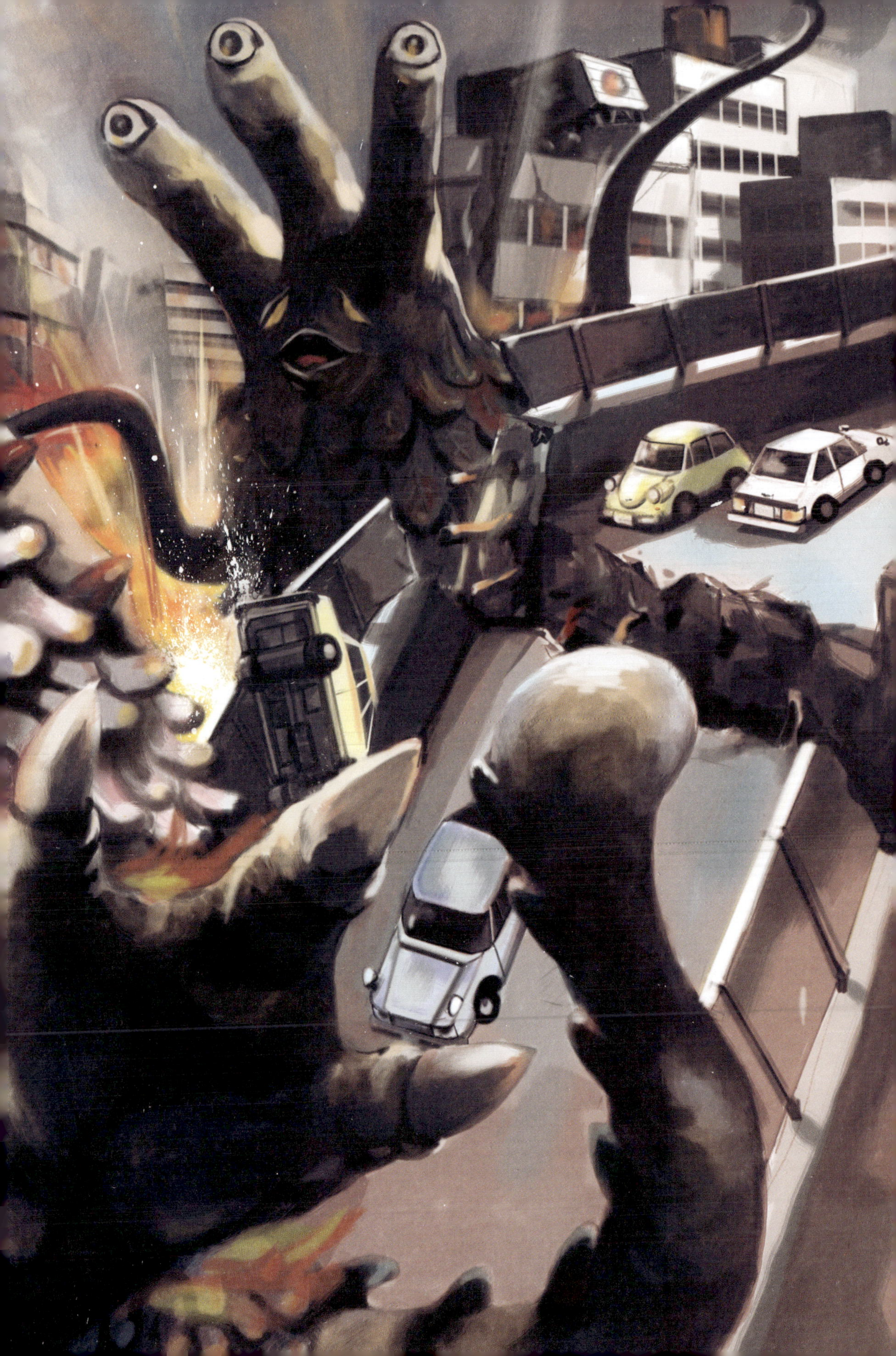

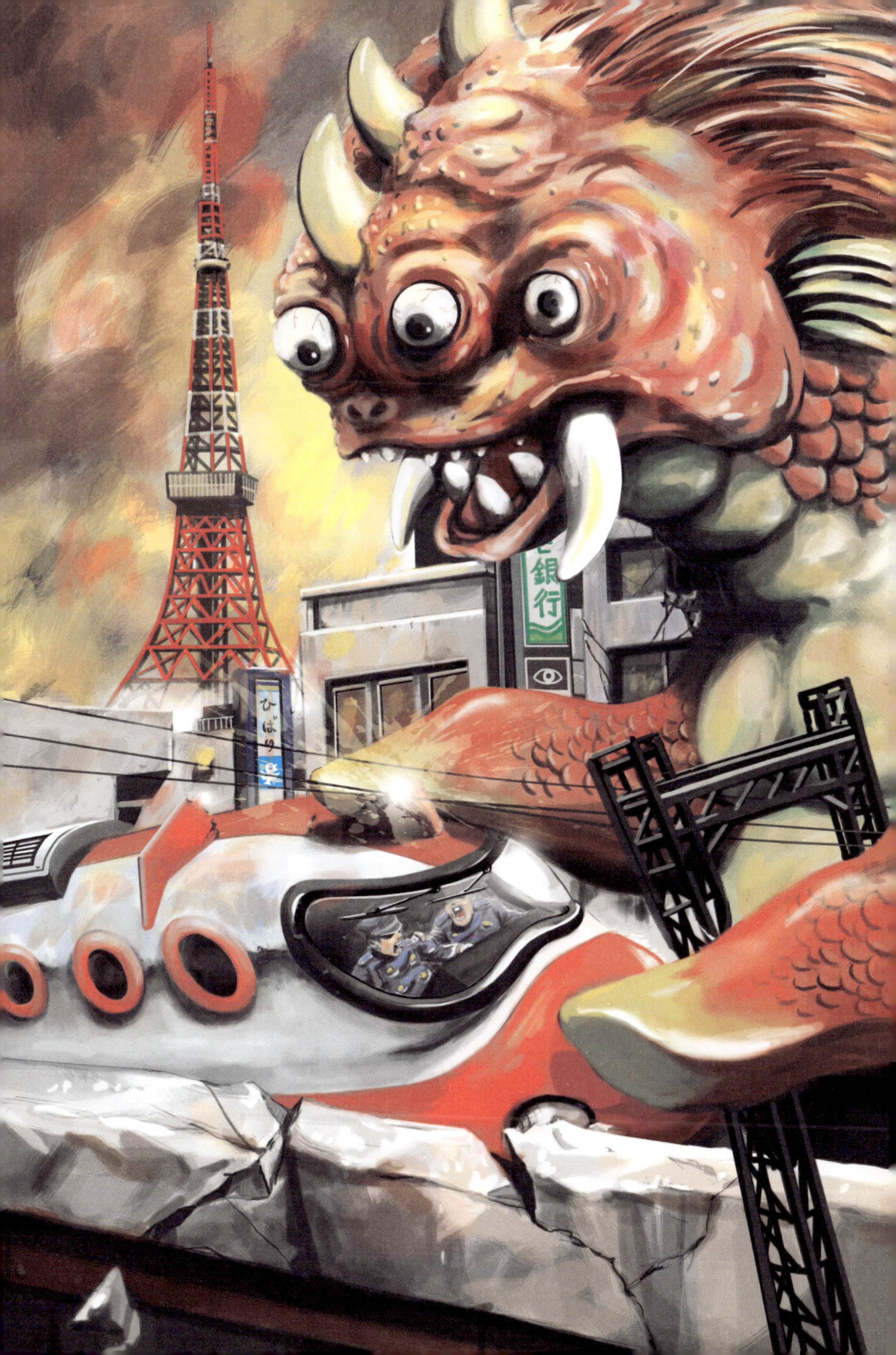
銀行
ひばり

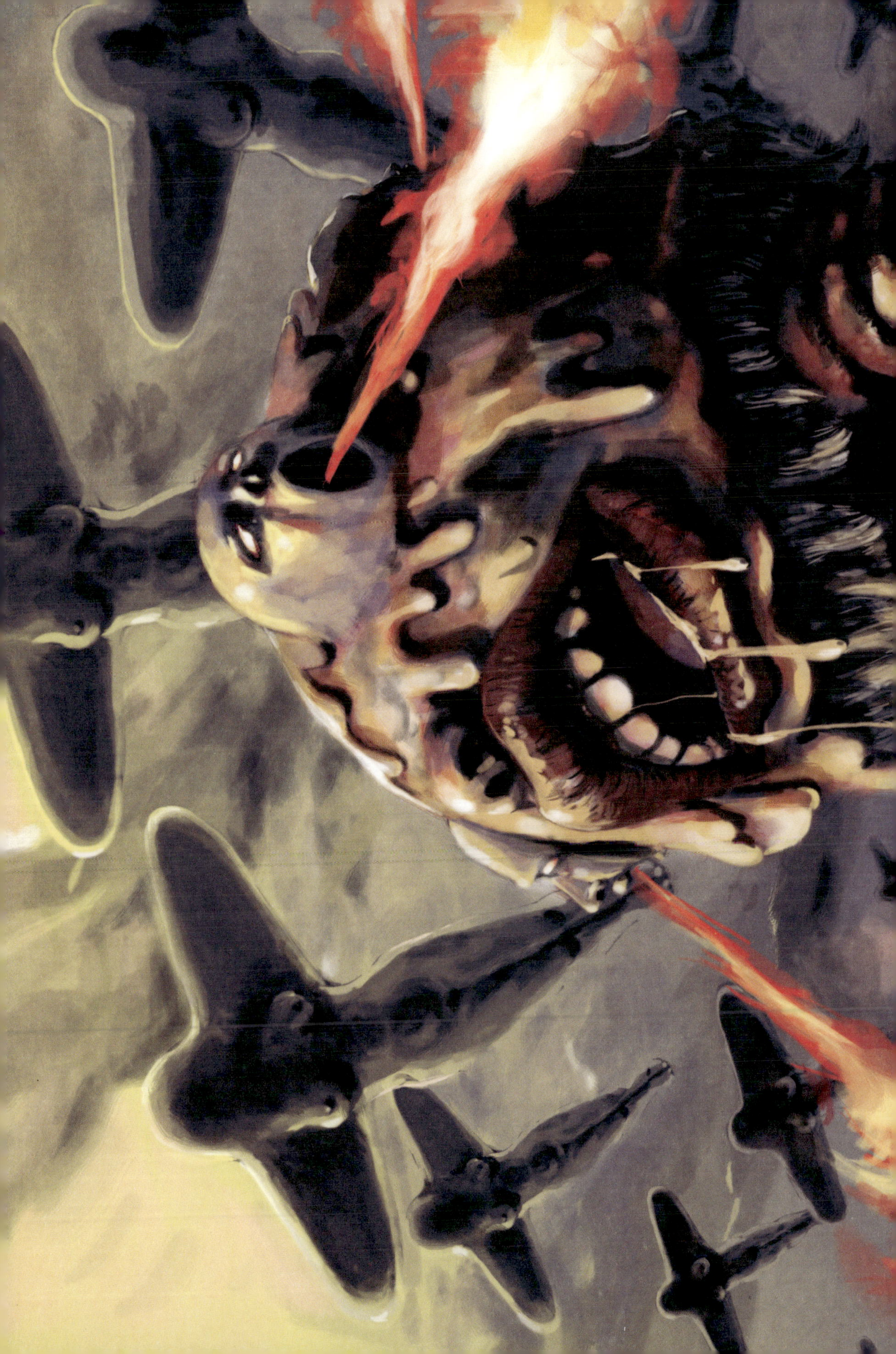

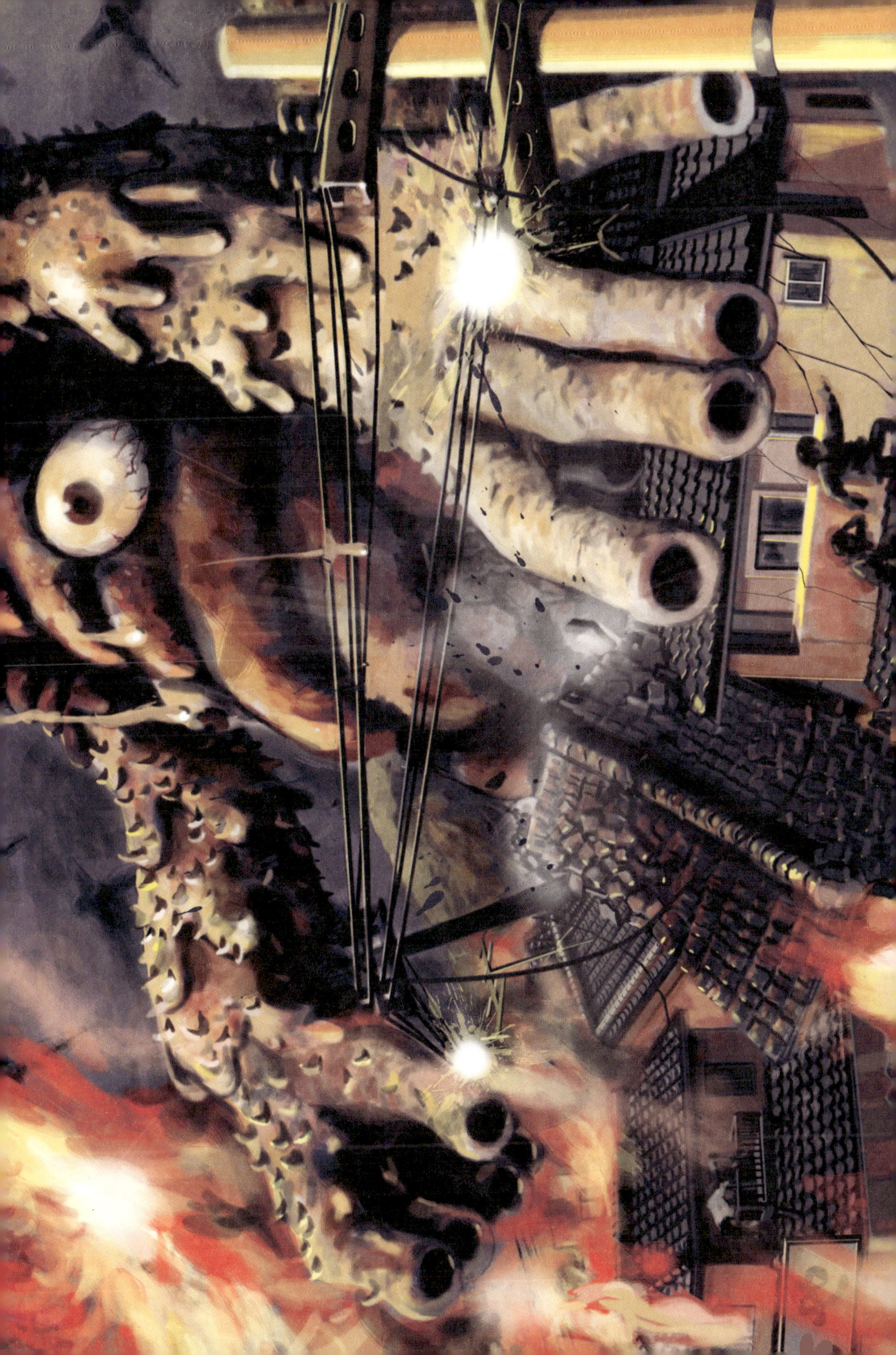

怪獣×妖怪

Kaiju vs. Yokai

Illustrations by Shinji Abe

The following comic dramatizes the thematic and stylistics differences between kaiju and yokai characters in postwar Japanese films and television productions. The divide between the two as illustrated here reflects the real-life division of the two genres as it existed during the 1960s and 1970s. To recreate the feel of Edo-period publications, traditional page sequencing has been used. The last page of the book is the first page of the comic.

Page 142–143: In the beginning, the cosmos was a unity of matter and spirit. Swirling cloudlike masses effortlessly shifted between states of transience, disembodied sentience, and corporeal incarnation. They existed in a state of pulsing flux—a perfect symbiosis of energies engendering a being that was a harmony of vessel and contents, a fluid interchangeability that blurred the lines of division and attachment.

Pages 140–141: The primitive inhabitants of the land were simple agrarians who respected the unnamed cosmic beings. The beings appeared as three-eyed amoeba-like shapes, floating about in the air, and were transparent at times. The world around these early people was suffused with the peaceful presence of the cosmic beings. All was serene.

Pages 138–139: In time these simple people who had subsisted on the bounty of their lands developed a more advanced civilization. Sadly, with their new but limited understanding many were gripped by confusion and fear. As their civilization developed, lands that were once tilled and plowed were paved over. Tall buildings and endless networks of roads and tunnels disturbed the habitat of the cosmic beings. The agitation of these beings reignited man's ancient fears. What were these speechless beings floating around? What did they want? Why do they appear? The tools men had once used to work the land became their weapons. As the first human fist was raised to strike a blow against these beings, a bolt of lightning ripped through the fabric of the world.

Pages 134–135: Some of these forms were extinguished as mysteriously as they appeared. Some perished, and those which remained survived somehow as severed halves. In time, these fragments developed, morphed in shape, and twisted with the untempered pain of their horrid division.

Pages 132–133: Prevalent among these misshapen creatures were what have come to be known as the Kaiju and the Yokai. The contempt they feel as a result of their treatment at the hands of humans has snuffed out all memory of how the cosmos was once at peace. With each generation their forms become more gnarled as their spirits harden. The Kaiju assumed flesh and bones—trapped as scaly and toothed predators, using might and roaring breath to stem the advances of man. The Yokai were obliged as spirits to creep from vessel to vessel, occupying whatever forms they could to survive.

Page 130–131: The Yokai inhabited the dark recesses of swamps and gutters or hid themselves in the mundane contrivances of civilization, slumbering for millennia, until one day they rampaged without cause or preamble. The people of the civilized world were thrown into a panic as inanimate objects started to hop around or writhe in place. Ghostlike shapes with long, snaking necks peered out of hairy heads with one eye.

Meanwhile, the streets were visited with devastation and turmoil. The Kaiju came from the waters, the mountains, and the sky to incinerate and reduce all structures to rubble. Their massive bodies thudded and shook the land with every step. Their shrieks were only muffled by the sounds of explosions or the crash of toppled buildings.

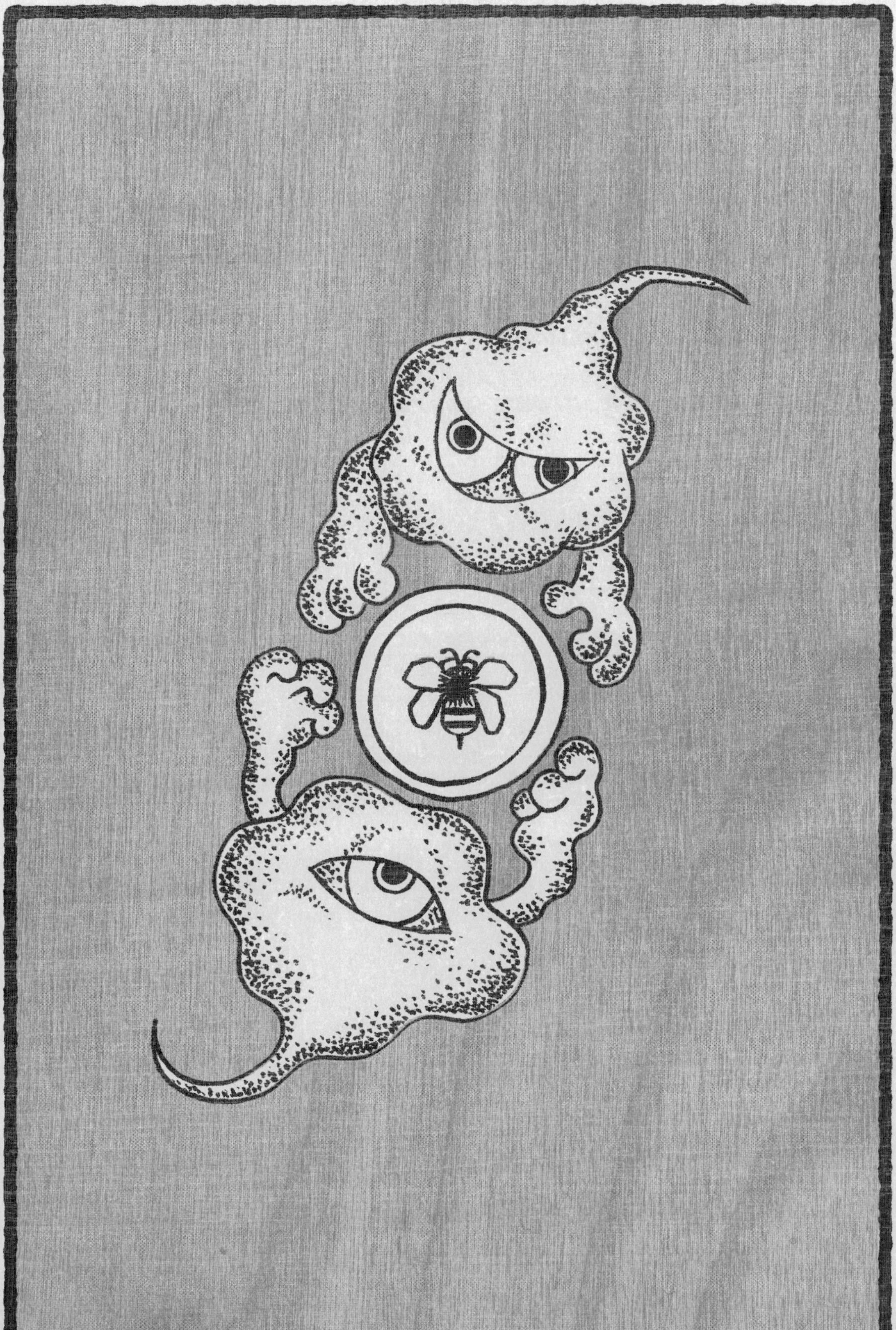

ふたたび
姿を現し
自らの領域を
侵したヒトへ
逆襲を
はじめるだろう

かつて地上を
追われた
怪獣と妖怪は

百万年の
時を経て
ヒトはさらに
怪獣や妖怪たちの
領域にまで
踏み込みはじめた

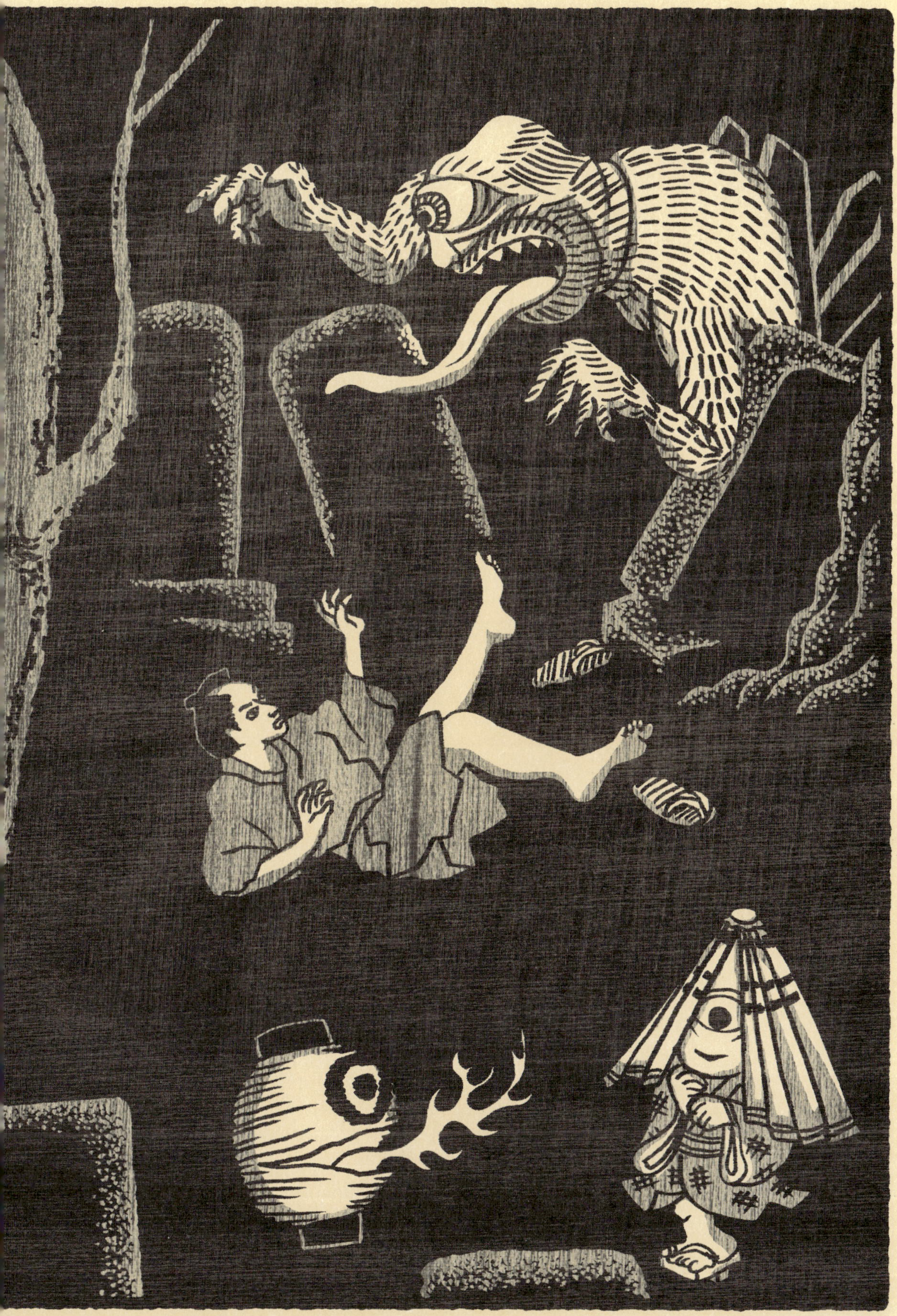

妖怪

ヒトやモノのような姿をしているが霞のように実体がない念の力で呪いをかけたり災いをもたらしたりする片目から髪や首が長いものやまたはモノに憑くものがいる

- ロクロクビ
- カッパ
- ソウゲンビ
- ノッペラボウ
- ツクモガミ

恐竜のような姿で
骨や内臓があり
実体がある

獣のような
鳴くものもいて
特殊な力を使って
攻撃する

山くらいの巨大なものまでいる
体は家くらいのものから

シッポ
ツメ
カタイヒフ

怪獣

長い時間をかけて姿を変えていった

海と宇宙に
逃れた体は怪獣へ
あの世に
逃れた魂は
妖怪へと

ヒトに
追われ
地の果てまで
逃げてカミは
雷に打たれて
体と魂を二つに
裂かれた

やがてヒトは
知識を
得ると
不思議な
力を持つカミを
地上から追放して
世界を自分のものに
しようとした

地上に住むものはヒト
天上や冥界を行き来するものはカミと呼ばれ
それらは共に暮らしていた

冥

天

地

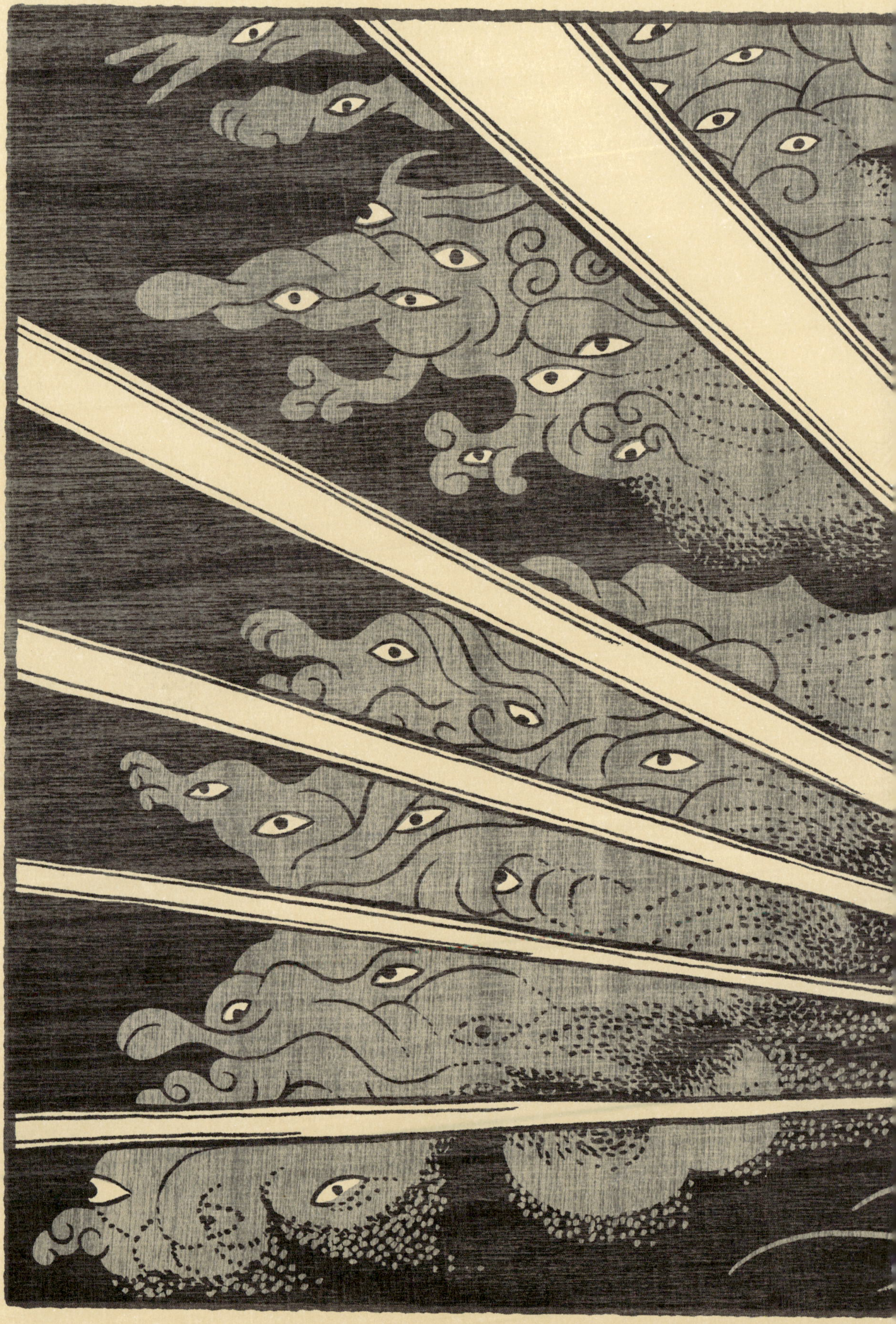

はじめ世界は
ひとつの
混沌であった
やがて光が
生まれると
秩序ができ
それぞれは
別の形と
成していった

彼等(カレラ)作(サク)

怪(かい)獣(じゅう)妖(よう)怪(かい)仇(あだ)討(うち)伝(びん)

版元(ハンモト) 悟理我出版(ゴリーガシュッパン)